Dear Al-Qaeda:

Letters to the World's Most Notorious
Terror Organization

DEAR
AL-QAEDA

Letters to the World's Most Notorious
Terror Organization

Scott Creney

Black Ocean
Boston · New York · Chicago

Copyright © 2006 by Black Ocean

To reprint, reproduce, or transmit electronically, or by recording all or part of *Dear Al-Qaeda*, beyond brief excerpts for reviews or educational purposes, please send a written request to the publisher at:

BLACK OCEAN
P.O. Box 990962
Boston, MA 02199
www.blackocean.org

ISBN 978-0-9777709-1-5

Library of Congress Cataloging-in-Publication Data

Creney, Scott, 1972-
Dear Al-Qaeda : letters to the world's most notorious terror organization
/ by Scott Creney.
p. cm.
1. Qaida (Organization)--Humor. I. Title.
PN6231.Q35C74 2006
816'.6--dc22
2006000925

Printed and bound in the United States of America.

FIRST EDITION

Maya Jade Connelly is a genius, and without her
this book would not exist.

Dear Reader.

First off, the bible quotes scattered throughout this book are from the King James version I bought at Dollar Tree. If your bible is a different translation, then that's just your tough luck.

So about the book you're holding: you probably won't find any of this funny at all. That's okay. A sense of humor, like beautiful children or a friendly dog, is something that all good Americans like to think they possess. In my experience, unfortunately, most do not.

If you're one of those people who is offended by words & ideas that you don't care for, and yet still insist on reading this book anyway–a book likely to make you very very angry, then I believe you're part of the greatest problem we face on this planet: ignorance. And I hope Al-Qaeda reserves a special place for you in their latest schemes. And I hope this book makes you weep.

And I hope you ask yourself why you find such pleasure in making yourself angry.

Love,

Scott

"HaHaHaHaHaHaHaHaHa"

–the final episode of *Everybody Loves Raymond*
broadcast May 16, 2005

Dear Al-Qaeda.

I spend my days. I reminisce while time is running out. Fiddling, burning. You know this letter is just me trying to convince myself that any of this matters.

I mean, what with television and the war and all.

Outside my window, faceless cars go back & forth. Further up the street, the owner of the Villa Nova motel and his wife, from a country somewhere east of Iraq and west of Thailand, go back & forth–through the various rooms, pushing supply carts and vacuum cleaners. The sun goes back & forth across the sky. The record needle goes back & forth across the various slabs of vinyl rescued from my car in the wilting Florida October heat. Me, I never go back or forth.

Forget back. Forget forth. I don't even go. I stay. I sit. I sediment.

Oh hell just take my hand and we'll sing etcetera.

See you on the other side and other such small comforts.

Dear Al-Qaeda.

Your number isn't listed in the phone book. I'm afraid to try and find you on the internet; Al-Qaeda-related web-sites are now monitored by the government for suspicious activity. If I shout your name out my window, the people walking on the street below will dive for cover.

I hear Guantanamo Bay is very . . . *gulag*-ish this time of year.

Still, I feel I must address you directly, Al-Qaeda, for it appears we have something in common. The United States of America is pissing me off and nobody will listen.

Just look at the television. And why not, when television is the place where real life happens and real life is the place where we all watch television.

The news programs make me furious. The unbiased anchors surrounded by their experts. They are experts because they are rich, because they wear a tie. But never a housekeeper to talk about the economy. Or a construction worker. Or even, like me, a caterer.

In the best of times, this would be considered amusing. Today, when so much is at stake in our nation, it, um . . . makes you want to kill somebody.

The entertainment programs are just as bad. VH1 and their relentless analysis of decades. *I Love the 80's. I Love the 90's.* They have a new show now called *Best Week Ever* which might as well be called *I Love This Week.* MTV and their spoiled children jostling to be famous for something, anything. They don't want to be famous because of their talent. They want to be famous because they want to be special, because they can never be special unless television says they are.

I'm here to tell you, Al-Qaeda, they are not special. They are average. They are spectacularly average. Even in their beauty, which meets our current standards of television beauty, they are average. But then maybe the point isn't to be beautiful, maybe it's just to look like the people who are already there. Maybe they believe becoming a celebrity is as simple as looking like a celebrity. Like looking like a quarterback, or a plumber, or a terrorist.

The rest of the channels are filled with comedy shows that aren't funny. Dramatic programs that aren't dramatic because everybody knows the cop will catch their criminal or the marital problem will be resolved. Market research shows that the audience wants their happy endings, and a happy audience means higher ratings which means more advertisers which means more money which means everything.

To quote the book everyone here seems so fond of quoting, ". . . vanity of vanities; all is vanity." That's from Ecclesiastes, a book in the Holy Bible. It goes on:

> *To every thing there is a season, and a time to every purpose under the heaven: A time to be born, and a time to die; a time to plant, and a time to pluck up that which is planted; a time to kill, and a time to heal; a time to break down, and a time to build up . . .*

Most people recognize that passage from the Byrds song, "Turn Turn Turn," or the John Grisham book *A Time To Kill*, or from Footloose—"and a time to dance, that time is now." Read that passage again Al-Qaeda, you kill and break. In response, we kill and break. I see this happening and it makes me want to kill someone too; it looks like fun. But unlike you or my country, I am not allowed to kill.

So when comes the time to heal?

I try to tell people about the way I feel, watching the television, yelling at the television, shaking with anger. They all think I'm crazy. They don't understand why I would put my faith in MTV or CNN in the first place; why I even care. They tell me I should just accept the lies, the hypocrisy, the distance between our ideals and our actions because nothing is ever going to change. Tell me, Al-Qaeda, are these our only choices? Anger or cynicism?

Al-Qaeda, you have chosen anger. You have chosen to try and change the world, and though I hope you never succeed—for I do not wish to live under a theocracy, though some might say I already do when a man can't stand in the White House without first dropping to his knees and begging for god's infinite mercy (a mercy which seems all too finite in these godless days). I may not agree with your goals, but I share your outrage at Western culture and what it has become. I repeat, it seems you and I have something in common, Al-Qaeda. The wish to see this culture permanently changed for the better.

Perhaps we can work together, until our paths diverge. I hope this letter finds you well, wherever you may be. Though I worry you might be inside each of us already.

Dear Al-Qaeda.

I fucking hate. I fucking hate so much.

People who don't use their turn signal. People who drive too fast–who drive too slow. People who don't wave when I let them into traffic. People who play their music too loud at stoplights.

God, just driving. Driving, alone.

Watching the cars fly down U.S. 19 at 55 miles per hour makes me believe that if the speed limit on every road were lowered to 35, nobody would ever die in a car accident again. But we would rather die than be late to work, literally.

The people who drive the fastest are the ones with nowhere to go.

Al-Qaeda, I want you to turn our roads into thick black soup. Have you developed a heat ray yet? You could watch this whole fucking overpaved nation melt and sink back into the fossils it came out of.

Heat ray or no, you're coming for us. I've seen the Osama Bin Laden videotapes. But I have this question, and it won't go away: What the fuck have you guys been doing?

When I lived in Boston, 24 hours after September 11th, some friends and I spent the evening deciding how many more terrorist attacks would have to occur before we'd leave the city. After much debate, we agreed that two more terrorist attacks like 9/11, or three biological attacks, and

17

we were gone. We figured we wouldn't be spending Christmas in Boston.

But since September 11th, nothing. Someone sent anthrax in the mail, but that wasn't you. Someone began shooting random shoppers in the Washington D.C. area, but that wasn't you either.

I don't understand. What was all that talk about teaching us a lesson, teaching us to fear like the rest of the world fears, of bringing death and destruction to our front door the same way we've brought it to the rest of the world? Our leaders told us you were already living among us, that we needed to be vigilant, that our very survival depended on this vigilance. That we needed colors to tell us the correct level of vigilance to maintain.

I don't understand what you're waiting for. It doesn't take much to scare us. With some AK-47's you could easily co-ordinate a simultaneous attack on shopping malls around the country. Topple some hotel in Panama City Florida during spring break. Kill America's favorite racehorse or soap opera star. Kidnap the actor who played Mini-Me in those Austin Powers movies. Film yourselves gang-raping Julia Roberts (she's America's Sweetheart according to *Entertainment Weekly*). Hell, have you ever attended one of our sporting events, Al-Qaeda? You could get a weapon past security with no problem. Just last week, my girl-friend Maya snuck a subway sandwich into a Devil Rays game, and that's way bigger than a box cutter.

Listen, I'm not saying that you *should* kill any of these people. I'm just saying that it seems you are all talk and no action. An entire nation is waiting for the other shoe to drop and here you are walking around in flip-flops.

America's done everything it can to provoke you. Since

September 11th, if it worships Allah, we've either bombed it, killed it, deported it, imprisoned it, tortured it, or desecrated its holy books. We've increased aid to Israel; we even arrested Cat Stevens. If this was an old Bugs Bunny cartoon, we'd have slapped you in the face with an oversized white glove and challenged you to a duel a hundred times by now. Where is your manhood, Al-Qaeda? Are you muslim or are you mice?

Is this any way to make a nation of people cower in fear? I saw a story on the news today. They said you were planning to smuggle nuclear weapons from Europe into Mexico, then bring them across the Mexican border. Do you know what I did, Al-Qaeda? I shrugged my shoulders and laughed. At you, Al-Qaeda. So what are you gonna do about it?

That's what I thought bitch.

Dear Al-Qaeda?

Can I call you Al?

Paul Simon says I can call him Al, but insists that I be his bodyguard in return. Paul does say, however, that in addition to letting me call him Al, he will also be my "long lost pal"–whatever that is.

There is a catch. I have to let him call me Betty. I'm not sure how I feel about this, seeing how my name is Scott, a boy's name. The name Betty belongs to a girl, which I am not. Regardless, Paul keeps insisting I can call him Al. So why shouldn't I be able to call you Al as well, with Al at least being part of your name?

Please get back to me soon on this. I have many more letters to write, so in the interests of space etc.

Oh, and for what it's worth, he also talked a lot about something spinning in infinity, angels in the architecture and the like. I think Chevy Chase was somehow involved as well, though I believe that may have just been a bad dream.

Dear Al-Qaeda.

I understand a lot of you have been to college. Then you know how important it is to get a good education. Here in America, we essentially have three different types of colleges.

Community College costs about $1,000 a year. It's exactly like high school, only without all the smart people. They already left town to attend one of our better college options. Class discussions at a community college tend to drag unless the teacher is able to steer the conversation towards car engines or Saturday night.

State College costs around $10,000 a year and is like community college for people with better families. They generally start with "University of" and end with the name of their home state. The state is then followed by a city, to differentiate the college from the other state schools. As a general rule, the larger your town, the higher your school's status. So in California, someone who attends University of California-Berkeley will be considered smarter than someone who attends University of California-Davis, unless they're majoring in cows. Class discussions at a state school revolve around the weekend, which begins late Wednesday afternoon and ends on Tuesday morning.

Private University is the third type of college. These cost at least $20,000 a year. In order to get into one, you have to score higher than 1150 on your SATs and be able to complete a job application without making more than three mistakes. Or you can just have rich parents. Typically, class discussions involve students passionately defending ideas they overheard in class the week before. The word "discourse" is frequently substituted for the word "talk," and ideas like absolute truth are considered hideously outdated–which comes in handy when explaining to your professors why you haven't done any of their assignments for that semester.

What ties these three college-types together is the fact that *they all cost money*. Now, I know a lot of colleges–certainly the schools in Europe, possibly even the universities in your homeland–are paid for by the government, but we don't do that in this country. If we did that, then *everybody* would be able to go to college, and there'd be nobody left to join our army. So we created this thing called student loans, wherein various banks, and occasionally the government, loan you money to pay for your education on the premise that after obtaining a degree, you'll be able to take all the extra money you'll be earning and use it to pay back these student loans.

Now, Al-Qaeda, you might be saying to yourself, "What about scholarships and grant money?" Good question. At the beginning of every school year, the college's financial aid department presents you with a financial aid award, which includes grant money from the school and government. This amount varies from case to case, but as a general rule, the more money you're paying for tuition, the more money you'll be awarded. Either way, you have as much chance of getting the full amount covered as you do of winning the lottery.

Let's use me as an example . . .

COMMUNITY COLLEGE:
TUITION - $1,000   AWARD - $0   TOTAL COST - $1,000

STATE COLLEGE:
TUITION - $10,000 AWARD - $2,500   TOTAL COST - $7,500

So if I didn't want to attend community college–and I didn't, having already flunked out three times because I stopped showing up–a private school wasn't going to cost much more than a state school. So I decided to take the student loans, maybe procure some *additional* student aid, and get myself a decent education. Discourse. Discourse. Discourse. See, it worked.

Except for the *procure additional aid* part. It turns out that any additional scholarships would be deducted from my award. So if I found a scholarship for, say, 28-year-old Irish students from California which paid $1,000, that thousand dollars would then be *deducted* from the scholarship money my school had already awarded me. Pretty shitty, huh Al-Qaeda?

I know a lot of this is background and probably way more personal information than you need to know; but on the surface, student loan companies don't sound all that bad. They provide an opportunity for poor people to attend the college of their choice. I want you to know exactly who we're dealing with, Al-Qaeda, so you will understand why I hate these companies so.

Some more personal stuff. My father worked for the phone company his whole life. My mom drifted from retail store to retail store, usually as a manager. They divorced when I was eight. This was back in 1980, when divorce was still considered a sin. As the decade passed and divorce became more common, the Catholic church either changed their mind or decided to just let it go. Such is our country's commitment to the sanctity of marriage.

The point is I didn't grow up around a whole a lot of

money. By the time I decided to go to college however, my dad had retired from the phone company with a tidy pension. I won't go into the exact numbers, but when I was weighing the different colleges, my dad told me, "Don't worry about the money, the money's there. You go where you want to."

This doesn't sound like my father, but I swear I'm not making this up. We were walking up Newport Avenue in Ocean Beach, on our way to get *carne asada* burritos from Nico's taco shop.

Fast-forward five years. I've just gotten out of school, approximately $40,000 in debt. My job tutoring special ed students pays $10 an hour, and my dad's all up in my ass about the student loan people who keep calling his apartment. He says the stock market took a bunch of his money (some terrorist attack fucked up the economy), and that I need to face up to my financial responsibilities. Let's just say that at $10 an hour, I could barely face up to my rent, let alone $40,000 of debt.

Since then, my dad and I haven't spoken in nearly two years. In that time, I've drifted from job to job, trying to find something that will pay me a living wage, let alone allow me to start paying back my loans. Now I'm living in Florida because it seems that working as a caterer—as a fucking *caterer*, Al-Qaeda, I have to wear a bow tie and everything—might earn me enough money to send one of the books I've written in the last couple of years off to New York City where some publisher might buy it. This is what I've been reduced to, Al-Qaeda, the writing degree equivalent of scratch tickets.

I don't even have my diploma yet. The school says I owe them $300 for graduation ceremonies, which I did not attend. As soon as I have an extra $300, I have every intention of getting my diploma out of hock.

So I was thinking, since you guys are going to be attacking us anyway, why not attack somewhere that might . . . oh, how can I put this . . . somewhere that would benefit both of us. Or at least me.

No, not just me. That would be selfish. Why not attack somewhere that would benefit *all* the under-privileged college graduates in this great–I mean, in this repulsive, great satan, infidel-nation. Yeah. Fuck yeah. Did I mention there were a lot of middle-eastern students at my college? They said they were from Persia, but now we know better. They were probably from Iran. Maybe even Saudi Arabia. One girl was definitely from Afghanistan. In fact, she said she was the princess of Afghanistan. So as you can see, Al-Qaeda, we travel in the same circles, you and I. Two degrees of separation. We're almost like cousins or something.

There's this woman named Sallie Mae. She runs one of the largest student loan companies in the country, and she sends me more mail than my mom does. According to her latest letter, she's living in a place called Iowa City. Sallie with an 'e.' Mae with an 'e.' You know what to do. That death and destruction thing you do so well. Thanks.

Also, you did a pretty good job on that World Trade Center, but let's put you to the test, Al-Qaeda, just how much *do* you hate financial institutions? There's this company called Citibank, the ones who kept calling my dad, and they're the biggest dicks of all. Anyway, I think they have a headquarters in New York City so you wouldn't even have to buy a new map or anything. Again, I can get specific addresses if you need them, but I'd have to call Citibank to do that, and I'm reluctant to let them know where I'm living right now unless I know you're gonna come through for me.

If I could be so bold as to address your leader directly . . . Osama Bin Laden, I understand that you are also estranged from your father. And though you and your dad may never again kick the soccer ball around, understand that I am giving you and your followers an opportunity to allow a certain father and son to be able to watch a Red Sox spring training game together this March–the World Champion Boston Red Sox at that.

Not that you need more motivation, but did you know that the largest investor in Citigroup, of which Citibank is a subsidiary, is the Saudi Arabian royal family? Those traitors. You must hate that. Sometimes I tell people that I'm not paying my student loans to protest this involvement. It's a bunch of bullshit of course, but it sounds good, and it makes other people feel bad about themselves for being a bunch of sellouts. Guilt can be such a powerful force. I understand it's how you come by most of your donations.

To sum up: kill Sallie Mae, kill Citibank. Nothing to it. Most days, you guys probably inflict more terrorism than that by your lunch hour. No need to respond. I'll be the one watching my television with breathless anticipation–even more so than usual.

Your comrade in death,
Scott

Dear Al-Qaeda.

My girlfriend and I are driving past the airport today on the way out to her mom's house, when she spots a plane coming in for a landing.

"I hope that motherfucker crashes," she says.

I'm not sure what she means by that, or maybe I'm just not able to process it, but I respond by telling her a story about my friend Alex. This was back in Boston, about a week after September 11th, and Alex and I had been up all night writing and playing video games; it seemed appropriate at the time. Neither one of us was ready to go to sleep, so when the Dunkin Donuts across the street opened at 5:30 in the morning, we were the first customers.

From my living room window, sipping our Great Ones, we watched the early morning planes fly in and out of Logan Airport. We could see the Prudential Center and the John Hancock Tower extend into the sky, and from the perspective of my 2nd floor apartment, each approaching plane looked to be heading straight for the skyscrapers. Alex began to root for each plane to clear the buildings. *Come on, come on, you can make it.* As each one approached, we would take a breath and hold it until the plane safely passed. Then we would laugh hysterically.

After a while, our game started to get old. So we began rooting for the planes to hit the buildings instead. *A little to the left, come on Mohammed, you can do it.* For whatever reason, this version of the game was more fun.

"Damn, he made it!" my girlfriend shouts.

My girlfriend has a name: Maya. Her middle name is Jade, and she is every bit as lovely. We've been living together for a few months now, and this is more than love. It is us against the world, and the world won't be winning for much longer. We are partners, sidekicks, inseparable.

You'd probably like her, Al-Qaeda. Despite being a mix of Irish and German, she has olive skin and her eyes look vaguely Mediterranean. Middle-Eastern people frequently mistake her for one of their own. Back when she was waitressing at Macaroni Grill, one customer told Maya that she'd be treated like royalty in India or Pakistan, where her lighter skin color would imply a more privileged background.

I ask Maya about the plane, about rooting for it to crash, if it's some kind of defense mechanism from September 11th.

"Fuck no. Are you kidding? I'm not worried about that plane hitting anyone–except us, of course." She keeps watching the plane, tightening her grip on the car's door handle each time the plane wobbles. "I did not give a fuck about September 11th then, and I could give even less of a fuck about it now."

"That's right," I remember, "you were already in Boston then." We met in Boston, the April after 9/11.

"Yeah, and I was totally pissed that day too. It was like the first day off I'd had in a month–I was working all these hours at Fire & Ice and between that and school, it was ridiculous. So I had a *thousand dollars in cash*, and was going to blow all of it shopping. My big day. And I'm getting off the subway that morning and walking around when I find out that all the stores are closing because someone just flew a plane into the World Trade Center.

And I was confused–because Boston has a World Trade Center–and I hadn't noticed someone flying a plane into anything and I probably would have noticed that–but then I found out it was the one in New York and then I just got confused."

"Right. I did the same thing. One guy actually told me it *was* the World Trade Center in Boston."

"But I was fucking pissed. Because they'd just ruined my day off, my *one* day off that month. And listen, we can feel bad for all the people who died, but I didn't know any of them. And you know what, I'll bet you that more people died on September 10th than September 11th, because everyone went home after the attacks and just stayed inside. But we don't stop and have moments of silence for any of *those* motherfuckers who died on September 10th. And if I fucking died that day, none of them would've cared about me."

"True."

"Anyway, I was hanging out with Rob later that night and I told him that was probably the coolest thing I'd ever heard of. I mean, to hijack a plane with a motherfucking boxcutter and directly hit the world trade center? That is some serious fucking balls. That shit takes balls the size of . . ."

"–The World Trade Center?" I interrupt.

She smiles. "The size of a *thousand* World Trade Centers. Those motherfuckers did not care *dick* about shit. I want to do that. Just take a plane and pull out a box cutter, not even a gun but a motherfucking *box cutter*, and tell everyone that I'm taking over the plane. And then fly that plane into a building, and not only put this huge-ass hole in it, but to put a hole there in such a way that the whole building just collapses into itself. I'm just saying respect is due. And you know what, if I'd grown up in some third world country, with bombs getting dropped on me and the United States getting all up in *my* shit, I'd have no problem justifying it either." She admires the next plane coming in, probably imagines it flying into the control tower. "Hijacking a plane? That's just about the hottest thing I've ever heard of. I mean who would you rather fuck? One of those terrorist guys, or some guy with feathered hair who flips burgers at Hardee's?"

I tried to explain to her that you are religious zealots, who probably hate opinionated women as much as the Christian religious zealots who already live here, but she just shrugged it off. She believes she could convince you, if given the chance.

If only all zealots were so easily convinced.

Dear Al-Qaeda.

Apparently, the only sane reaction to the knowledge that you are responsible for bombs falling on somebody's family (and granted this responsibility, in most cases at least, is indirect, i.e. I pay taxes) is to buy an American flag, or more precisely a decal with a picture of the American flag on it, and display it proudly in the back window of your car. Not the front window, because who cares about that? A car passing from the other direction would see it for a couple of seconds, if he saw it at all. No, put it in the rear window and make the car behind you fucking squirm at how much more you love your country than he does, riding stickerless in his Honda or Toyota or some other foreign car. Your sticker will announce *Bite My Patriotism* in a clear and confident voice.

Does Al-Qaeda make flags? What do they look like? Are there any t-shirts available for sale? I imagine this one would be a big seller:

You're Welcome
~ Al-Qaeda

That would be a funny t-shirt. We sell Jesus t-shirts that are funny, as well as America t-shirts, Jesus bumper stickers, America bumper stickers, even Jesus bibles if you can believe that. You should get on this train, Al-Qaeda. There is money to be made.

Maybe bumper stickers are too permanent for you. I mean,

sure patriotism is really popular right now, but what if it proves to be just a fad? Well then go buy a magnet. We sell one now that reads "Support Our Troops." I understand it's fun to slap it on the back of your car even as you vote against the guy who might actually bring them home and keep them from dying.

Dear Al-Qaeda.

A conversation I recently overheard:

"So your new job, you must watch a lot of television."

"A little. We only get a few channels. No cable and all."

"No cable? Who ever heard of a motel without cable? Even a shitty motel like yours."

"It's not *my* motel. And we do have cable. Only not in the lobby, just up in the rooms. It's not that bad. I mean, I don't even have cable in my apartment anymore."

"You're kidding."

"No, I'm serious. I had to get rid of it, and not just because I couldn't afford it. Cable was literally making me insane. I'd watch these cable news programs and it would just completely piss me off until I started screaming at these people to shut up."

"Screaming?"

"Red in the fucking face. Then change the channel and it's all these sports and entertainment channels, like VH1 counting down the 100 sexiest bass players of all time. I couldn't tell what was worse, those assholes on the news trying to push their pig-headed agendas or these other channels pretending that nothing out of the ordinary was even happening. War? What war?"

"And you're screaming all of this at your television. Alone."

"I'm telling you, if I watch cable tv for longer than an hour, I want to join Al-Qaeda–"

"You what?"

"–and help them destroy our shallow, decadent, culture."

"Al-Qaeda?"

"I'm *serious*. You watch this shit and Osama's speeches about 'decadent American culture' and 'the great satan' start to make sense. More sense than we make anyway. I mean, how can we sit here and talk about 'the dignity of life,' when I turn the channel and in the same breath see some cocktail waitress with a heart of gold getting her tits inflated."

"So because cable tv upsets you–"

"Fucking screaming."

"–you want to join Al-Qaeda."

"Look I know it sounds weird, but I'm serious. I even went and looked them up in the phone book the other night, just for kicks. Turns out they're not even listed, which makes you wonder how they plan to overthrow Western society if nobody knows how to join their secret club. Maybe there's some kind of underground code; this secret society that meets in public toilets at three in the morning. I thought about trying the internet, doing a google search for Al-Qaeda. They must have a website, right? Or a livejournal? Can't you picture their LJ? *Current mood: Terrorizing.* But yeah, a website, maybe with some Frequently Asked Questions. Links to some of their friends in other terrorist groups. A photo gallery . . ."

"I'm guessing you found none of this?"

"Didn't even look. I chickened out. I pictured myself in the library typing in 'Al-Qaeda' when suddenly all these sirens go off and stormtroopers pop out of the ceiling and slide down ropes to arrest me. If I was lucky, and I'm talking *lucky*, maybe I get a trial before getting shipped to Guantanamo."

"Right."

" . . . I wonder if it's fun being a terrorist."

"Fun?"

"Well compared to say, working the night audit at a motel."

"Nobody ever died from being a night auditor."

"Not true. Haven't you ever heard of Gary Gilmore?"

"Who?"

"Nevermind. Well, okay, maybe flying into a building isn't fun, but what about the rest of it. I bet the meetings must be really cool. Like Alcoholics Anonymous or something. 'My name is Steven, and I'm a terrorist.' Maybe that's it, someone has to sponsor you in order to join. But just think what that's like, eating a cheeseburger and you're a *terrorist*. Wouldn't that just absolutely blow your fucking mind? Or taking a shower. 'I'm a terrorist and I'm taking a shower.' That shit's crazy."

"Excellent choice of words."

"Well imagine those fucking World Trade Center guys. Everyone remembers that they flew out of Boston, but the week before they were all up in Portland staying in a hotel. I mean, have you ever been to Portland? Stores close real fucking early in Portland on a Sunday. What do you think they did to kill time? I mean, do you think they watched tv? cable? Were they calling up MTV to request a Britney Spears video, just to get in the mood to hate America enough to fly a plane into a building? That would be so awesome. Sitting in your hotel room, calling up room service, maybe studying some flight manuals. Do you think they swam in the hotel pool? I mean, *what do terrorists think*? Or maybe they went out. Maybe they hit the town. Picked up some prostitutes. Or they went to Papa Gino's. Fucking Al-Qaeda took a taxi to Papa Gino's and ordered a pizza. The girl behind the counter asks them if they want sausage on their pizza and they make this really pissed-off face, maybe even think about killing her right there, or flying one of those planes into Papa Gino's instead. But they can't get mad because it'll blow their cover, so they go and sit at their table and just *mock* America and its pizza. They probably call it 'infidel pizza.' I mean, wouldn't it be worth it, to join Al-Qaeda, just so you could call Papa Gino's 'infidel pizza?' They should really put that in their brochure."

"Al-Qaeda has a brochure?"

"Sure. Why not? Fuck, even the Hyatt where I used to work had a brochure. *You'll Love Our Spacious Rooms.*"

"Does the JackRabbit Inn have a brochure?"

"If we do, I'd try to avoid touching it. I mean without wearing gloves . . . Do you think terrorists jog?"

"Jog?"

"I'm just saying, if you knew you were going to fly a plane into a building, say . . . in a month, would you still exercise? Would you keep brushing your teeth? These are things I really think about. I would love to interview someone in Al-Qaeda, one of those guys down in Guantanamo Bay. I want to know what terrorists have for breakfast. I want to know if they ever go to McDonald's. All we ever hear about is the stuff they hate, but what do terrorists enjoy? Do terrorists ski? Skiing's not a sin, right? What do you think they do for fun?"

"I don't know . . . Torture?"

"See, I don't think it's like that at all, that they sit around pulling the wings off butterflies, or stapling caterpillars to chalkboards. I imagine at some point being a terrorist has to become just like any other job. Do you remember that old cartoon with Wile E. Coyote, where the coyote's trying to grab these sheep and the sheep dog keeps trying to stop him? Anyway, at the beginning of the cartoon the coyote and the sheep dog punch this time clock, like they're working in a factory, and when the whistle blows–it's out in the forest but there's still a factory whistle, it's attached to this tree–the coyote starts doing his job, which is to steal the sheep, and the sheep dog starts doing his job, which is to protect the sheep. Come to think of it, what the fuck is a coyote doing in a *forest*? Whatever. So when the whistle blows to take a break, they just stop what they're doing–usually the sheepdog is kicking the shit out of the coyote–and they go have a coffee break or lunch or whatever. And during the break they talk about how their wives and kids are doing, the weather, the whole bit. Then the whistle blows and they calmly walk back to where they were before and pick up where they left off. Then at the end of the workday they go and grab a beer together. Of course the coyote's covered with bandages, and he's got a broken leg and shit, but I imagine that being a terrorist is like that. They're just doing their job. When they're over here in America, they probably go to Tom Cruise movies and the mall and all that shit. Some of them probably enjoy it. Hell, they probably go to bars and get shit-faced every night. It's not like you have to get up early to start hating infidels."

"You know muslims aren't allowed to drink."

"What, do you think they're somehow *better* at being religious and holy than everybody else? The Bible forbids pre-marital sex, but that doesn't seem to stop anyone here. Hell, most of the time, the more righteous and holy you are on the surface, the more fucking sick you are underneath. You don't think there're muslim Jerry Falwells and Pat Robertsons out there? I worked with this one muslim guy, back when I was still at the Hyatt. He was from Morocco, and he used to bang anything that moved. And this guy was married for Christ's sake."

"For *Allah's* sake."

"For fucking Cookie Monster's sake. Whatever. I'm just telling you that no human being is perfect. And the one who *was* perfect became so perfect that they killed him as soon as they found out about it. I bet there's probably a terrorist somewhere paying someone this very second to shit into his mouth."

"So you want to be a terrorist . . . to have someone shit in your mouth."

"If I could just talk to one . . . You know what they should do? And I'll bet you even our current administration would love this. Whenever our military captures a terrorist, or even someone they suspect is a terrorist, they shouldn't kill him or torture him or any of that. What they should do is sell him.

"Sell him? You mean like a slave?"

"Slave makes it sound so dirty. I was thinking more like pets. But don't just sell them to one or two people, sell them to whole neighborhoods. Then the different neighborhoods could have little terrorist wars. Nothing too serious, maybe just have one terrorist toilet paper another terrorist's neighborhood, or blow up their garbage cans or something. It'd be a good way to make us feel more comfortable about terrorists, like the way little kids play with dolls to act out the stuff that scares them. Who knows, maybe people would start talking to their neighbors. Maybe it would create a sense of community, and we'd care about our fellow man again."

"And when exactly was this time when people cared about their fellow man?"

"I'm not—"

"Because it seems to me, looking back at history, that people have always been—"

"Yeah, but—"

"—pretty much inherently selfish."

"But," and with that he paused for a breath, "it couldn't always have been like this. Could it?"

Dear Al-Qaeda.

The last several nights, I keep waking up at 4:30 in the morning and I can't stop coughing. Maya eventually rolls over and exhales loudly to let me know she's annoyed that I woke her up. So I get out of bed and head into the kitchen to make myself a cup of this vitamin supplement called Emergen-C, and I sit at the kitchen table and read, usually a book or the back of a cereal box or something. I had really bad asthma when I was a kid, so I learned all these tricks to calm yourself down and help stop the coughing. One of these tricks was reading.

I sit in the kitchen, and after I finish the Emergen-C I spit my phlegm into the now-empty glass because it's not healthy to swallow your phlegm. When the cup becomes half-full with thick yellow-green mucus–or half-empty if you prefer, depending on the perspective of terrorists–my breathing is under control and I can go back to sleep.

I am wondering if you ever get sick Al-Qaeda, and if so, what kind of diseases you get. I imagine your immune systems are probably not well-equipped for living among the various pollutants of Western culture. You must sniffle a lot. Is this true? Like me, do you sometimes wake up at 4:30 in the morning unable to breathe? And if you do, do you ever find yourself wishing you were someplace else? Maybe back in your homeland, back in the desert, in a place that doesn't know words like ragweed or pollen? I wonder if you ever feel guilty in these moments, Al-Qaeda, when you're exhausted and coughing, far from home and wishing you'd never heard of freedom fighters or *jihads* or a strange place called America that keeps making you cough.

Dear Al-Qaeda.

24 million different Iraqis were just too much for us to take in all at once. Like trying to picture 24 million snowflakes, or 24 million shadows. So we turned them into one Iraqi. A Joe Iraq. Or a Mohammed Public if you prefer. The idea flowed back and forth between our federal halls and the office of whittled statistics until we had created one average Iraqi, assembled from spare parts.

A Joe Iraq torn against himself, pinching his left arm with his right and always attempting to kick himself in the head. A Joe Iraq with a Shiite arm and a Baathist toe. His left eye saw victory even as the right eye wept in defeat. From the waist down he thrashed in defiance, while his upper half, with the exception of a few stray chest hairs, supported the idea of a new democracy.

Still our thinking persisted. *If we can just unlock the secrets of Joe Iraq, we can unlock the entire country*, reasoned the white-washing rooms behind the District of Columbia doors, as our leaders searched for a domino effect we could all stand behind.

God, united. Life is precious and the Bible. Even as Joe Iraq begins chopping off limbs at a furious rate. Even as the heat hits the desert with an intensity that would fuse sand into jewelry were it not for the night. With each new color of glass one more warning for caution, our undyingly supported troops still sprint towards Joe Iraq and his skittish machete.

Dear Al-Qaeda.

We are dominated by a system, by an abstract form.

It is time everyone realized that we are already resisting.

Dear Al-Qaeda.

We moved to Florida this past October, a couple of months ago. Maya's from the area, and we were seriously short on cash, so we decided to move down here for the winter because the tourist season is busy in Florida and we would be able to save up enough money to move anywhere in the country–or out of the country–we wanted.

So we found a cheap studio apartment in downtown St. Petersburg and got jobs with Orange Blossom Catering, one of the oldest and most prestigious catering companies in the Tampa area, which is a little like saying that colon is one of the oldest and most prestigious forms of cancer.

It's not too bad. The money is good. Maya and I get to work together, and for the most part, it's a great bunch of people to work with. So much so that I'm not going to go into great detail about their lives, which I assure you are far richer and more interesting than what currently passes for life in our shopping mall culture. I will mention that my favorite person there is named Eggy. He is a dark-skinned muslim from Trinidad, who gave up beer for Ramadan and who everyone thinks is gay. I don't think you two would get along, despite the number of people who worry that he might be one of you.

Dear Al-Qaeda.

In my brief tenure at Orange Blossom catering, I have acquired more memories than someone who's worked a lifetime in data entry, or middle-management, or convenience store working, or even, dare I say it, terrorizing.

I have carried plates of *hors d'oeuvres* and champagne through the penthouse of the Florenzia building, one of the swankiest apartments in the area, and seen something that looked suspiciously like cocaine in one of the bathrooms. I have worked nearly a dozen weddings, and heard the same music at each of these weddings.

At one wedding, we saw a father slide his hands down the bride's back–his daughter's back–until they reached the shelf which was the top of her ass, and then rest them there for the duration of the traditional father/bride dance. I have seen another wedding couple distribute souvenir pink beer cozies which read "Jill & Tommy." I saw one bride's mother tell the director of the Snell Isle Women's Club that she wanted all the pictures of the former Snell Isle Women's Club presidents–women with names like Thelma and Marge–to be taken down for the duration of the wedding. When the director refused, the mother retaliated by placing large, extravagant bows over each picture, blocking the presidents' faces from view. I still have no idea why.

Once, while standing in Dollar Tree with Maya, the song "Celebration" by Kool and the Gang began playing over the store's radio. I remembered a wedding we'd recently worked, and the fat, nine-year-old girl with blonde, stringy hair dancing with her grandfather, as he stumbled, tripped, and basically struggled to remain upright while trying to reconcile the shuffling of his feet with a full gin & tonic in his left hand.

Every wedding DJ will say he's not going to play "The Electric Slide." Do not believe him, Al-Qaeda. He is a liar, as all wedding DJs are liars. If you ever cater, do not be friendly to wedding DJs; they are never the caterer's friend.

Maya got to serve the President. There was this Republican fundraiser being held at one of the local mansions and for some reason I didn't get scheduled for that party. Karl Rove was there, as were the president and his brother Jeb, the governor of our sunshine state. Though he ate the same food as everyone else, George W. Bush had his personal secret service man prepare his plate and serve him. He didn't eat much of his food, just picked at the salad.

After the food was served, Maya and the rest of the caterers were instructed by the secret service to go and stand in the garage while George W. Bush delivered his campaign speech. It lasted for an hour. The garage was not air-conditioned, and at no point during the event did either the President or the Governor stop in to say hello. Maya did get some revenge though. When she picked up the empty plate next to him, George grinned at her, but she just scowled back at him and rolled her eyes. "He got a confused look after that and went right back to talking," says Maya.

I attended the year-end celebration for the race car drivers at DeSoto Speedway, and actually left disappointed because, unlike last year's award ceremony, none of the drivers got drunk and punched their pregnant wife in the stomach.

I have served several hundred swedish meatballs and brought the uneaten ones back to Orange Blossom after an event, only to serve them again two days later. I thought they tasted almost as good the second time.

I attended a party for the United Negro College Fund where each of the 300 attendees asked for a to-go box, proving once and for all that a ham is a terrible thing to waste.

I tended bar at a house party held in another of the many mansions that line the Tampa Bay coast and was forced to sing by a few of the older gentleman at the party. The lyrics?

> *We like to go swimming*
> *with bow-legged women*
> *and swim between their legs, hey!*
> *And swim between their legs, hey!*

After each *hey!* we downed another shot of whiskey. At the end of the night, they tipped me $150. This means they are good people.

After all this time, however, there is still one thing I can't figure out. No matter how poorly the event is run, all of these people seem to have the time of their lives. They see the walls decorated in pink & aqua blue, they see the white Christmas lights lining the ceiling, and they consider this beautiful, if not breathtaking. We, the caterers, laugh at the napkins we fold until they look like seashells. We laugh at the fake flower centerpieces, and around the holidays, we laugh at the reindeer skeletons made out of wicker. The people we serve love all of it, Al-Qaeda, they actually gush.

So here's the question, the thing I can't understand.

Who is sadder, them for finding this so beautiful, or me for mocking their enthusiasm?

The question alone makes me sad.

Anyway, in five months, we should be able to save a couple grand. Or what you probably receive in a day, Al-Qaeda.

And unlike you, all we needed to kill were small parts of ourselves.

Dear Al-Qaeda.

We were driving north along the interstate last week, and every town I passed through had lots of McDonald's-type restaurants and gas stations lining the freeway. In many of these towns, I could see churches as well.

The signs along the highway rose higher than the steeples.

I am not a religious person, and this shouldn't be considered as one more argument in favor of a theocracy, but I still think this means something. And what it means cannot be good.

Please write back soon. Nobody here will talk to me about this.

Your pal,
Scott

Dear Al-Qaeda.

I drift when I drive. Not enough to swerve or draw anyone's attention, but I still find my thoughts occupied by
everything except the road.

Here, clouds move at different speeds. One day a bunny,
the next day a turtle. What are clouds like where you live?
I'm not asking for clues, for you to reveal yourself, I am
merely curious.

And, on some days, if I drifted into another lane I don't
think I'd really mind.

In my late teens & early twenties, when I had nothing to
live for and nothing to lose, I used to root for an earthquake to come along and wipe out everything. All the 7-
11s and gun shops, the school buses and the national debt.
All of it. Gone. Please.

Because I grew up in California, I prayed for an earthquake. I've met people from Florida who wished for hur-
ricanes. People in Kentucky dream of tornados. Because
when you're young, when you're confronting the world
with new eyes, everything seems so broken and corrupt
that it'd be easier to just destroy everything and try to start
over.

We had an election last week, Al-Qaeda, an election for
President. You might have heard about it. Everyone wondered who you wanted to win. In the end, the experts on
television decided you'd rather see John Kerry become
president, because George Bush is willing to do whatever
it takes to fight terrorism. Whether Bush's efforts have

made us any safer is, at the very least, open to debate. No matter. It is his willingness to stand behind his decisions, even in the face of criticism–even in the face of galling evidence that he may be at fault–which proves he is more committed to fighting terrorism than John Kerry, who is less committed. Or would be, if he were president. 51 percent of voters thought so, at least.

But don't start patting yourselves on the back for influencing the election of the most powerful person in the most powerful country in the world. The real issue that decided this election is homosexuality. No, neither of the candidates have an "eye for the straight guy." John Kerry just thinks gay people should have the same rights as heterosexuals. The majority of Americans, apparently, disagree. Because homosexuality is a sin. This they know, because the Bible tells them so.

Closer inspection of the Bible, however, reveals that it isn't considered a major sin. No more a sin than, say, masturbation. In fact, there are seven sins so sinful that they are called "deadly sins." As of this writing, none are against the law.

In no particular order, the Seven Deadly Sins:

1. Pride
2. Envy
3. Anger
4. Sloth
5. Greed
6. Gluttony
7. Lust

Now let's consider these one at a time. Since we as a nation are so committed to the prevention of sin, I mean, as a culture and all. For argument's sake, we can estimate

51

what percentage of Americans engage in each sin.

Pride.

Can't mention America these days without the word pride following right behind it. American Pride. Used to sell everything from the trucks we drive to the bumper stickers we put on those trucks. Even the mothers I saw on Maury Povich today, the ones with the obese toddlers, told us how proud they were of the dozen ribs their babies could consume in one sitting.

And let's consider this sin's opposite: Shame. It would appear we live in shameless times. Planes are hijacked and flown into buildings. Our government fails to protect us and nobody resigns. Prisoners are tortured, violating international law. Nobody resigns. Rigged elections? Caught lip-synching? Don't resign. Fuck, don't even apologize. To apologize is to admit you did something wrong. To admit you were wrong is to admit weakness, and weakness is shameful. And we must never be ashamed. Ever. For to be ashamed means to not be proud, which means to not be an American. Which would be shameful, not to be from America, the greatest nation to ever nation its way across the earth.

Verdict. 50%. It would be higher but most women have been convinced they shouldn't be proud of the way they look. Especially the ones who are fat and ugly.

Envy.

Are you more beautiful than me? Do you have more money than I do? Are you more famous than me? Even if you're famous for being a drug addict with a failing marriage, I still wish I was as famous as you. And as beautiful. And had as much money. I like your car too. How come your girlfriend has bigger tits than mine? And wow, your house is so big. I want to just sit in front of the tv and watch people who are more rich and beautiful than I am talk about a bunch of really dumb bullshit. That would be awesome. Because I envy them so much. What's that? You say these tv shows already exist? What time are they on? By the way, did you see my neighbor's new car?

Verdict: 90%

Anger.

Close to home, we could look at road rage. Further from home, we could talk about Fallujah. Still closer to home, I could choose these letters, for it seems that I too am angry.

Still, most of us are too scared to actually act on our anger, at least in public, away from our loved ones.

Verdict: 65%

Sloth.

Even college students, our so-called best and brightest, seem incapable of putting down the bong or Xbox controller long enough to actually read the books their parents are paying $20,000 a year for them to study. Did I mention that I've worked about a hundred hours in the last four months? That averages out to less than ten hours a week. And all I've accomplished is a series of letters to a terrorist organization. And we don't even own an Xbox. Or marijuana.

Verdict: Whatever.

Greed.

Envy's next-door neighbor. Greed is Envy when Envy decides to stop being Slothful and actually do something about it. Envy with a purpose. Does voting Republican because they'll give you a tax cut, despite the fact that it will make the lives of your fellow Americans a good deal shittier, qualify as Greed? I believe it does.

Verdict: 51%.

Gluttony.

Fat Americans. Fat, bovine Americans with their cascading multiple chins. Like rings in a tree trunk, it seems we get an extra chin every ten years. Whether pounding their 7th Diet Coke of the day because they're counting calories, or becoming even unhealthier as they chase the latest fad diet, the gluttons of America need to take a good look in the mirror. Assuming they can find one large enough.

Verdict: After walking around the Pinellas Park Wal-Mart last Saturday afternoon, I'd have to put the number somewhere between 94 and 97%.

Lust.

Lust is one of the more dependable deadly sins. Without it, advertising culture and teen-pop sensations would cease to exist.

Verdict: 100%. Even Britney Spears, the last American spokesperson for virginity, got knocked up by a guy nicknamed "Cletus," who walked out on his child and pregnant girlfriend to be with her.

Listen, I understand that you can't make an ideology omelette without breaking a few hypocritical eggs, but to deny a group of people their civil rights *simply because the Bible considers them sinners*, seems a little . . . oh how should I put this? Fucked. And to re-elect a president–to ignore four years of systematic corruption and ineptitude simply because he also wants to deny this group their civil rights as guaranteed under the constitution–seems as completely fucked as anything you could ever hope to do in the history of elections. Please stop thumping your Bibles long enough to actually open up the fucker and read it.

Let he who is without sin cast the first stone. That is, if he's not too slothful to pick it up.

Oh, and Al-Qaeda, I haven't forgotten you guys either. I've read the Koran three times, and I can't find the words *jihad* or *hijack* in there anywhere. It would seem believing in superheroes who live in the sky and arguing over which one's stronger isn't getting us anywhere. We are proud, greedy, lustful, gluttons. All of us, every one.

Even the bone smugglers and turd burglars who plague middle-america's nightmares. I pray for earthquakes and they fear gay marriage; both of us are crazy. Nobody knows why.

Dear Al-Qaeda.

Do any of you have children?

Here in America, even the most pious among us have a tendency to sin. Recently, some of our priests, the people who are our direct access to God, were convicted of engaging in sexual relations with children. Do you like that phrase, engage in sexual relations with children? It sounds clean, doesn't it. Tidy.

If we were to be more accurate, if we were to say, "Priests shoved their cocks into the mouths and assholes of little boys," people in America would be offended. Probably more offended by my vulgarity and bad taste than by the actions of the priests themselves.

I saw a picture in the paper this morning of a child killed last week when American forces attacked Fallujah in Iraq as part of Operation Phantom Fury, a phrase that sounds like some DC Comics plot-line. Anyway, this child had been killed to the point where he looked more like a very bloody brussel sprout than a child. All because we are attacking insurgents in Fallujah who are trying to prevent the spread of freedom throughout Iraq.

I was not aware the situation over there had become so bad that the four-year-olds are against us as well.

According to a jury of his peers, the only crime Michael Jackson may have committed involves making shitty music for the last twenty years. He was accused of 'molesting' a boy–another nice, polite word. His defense, which basically amounted to "Hey, we may have slept in the same bed together, but nothing happened," was apparently convincing enough to avoid prison.

They make jokes about Michael Jackson–Jay Leno, David Letterman, and the rest–because apparently pedophilia is funny now. Let's have a chuckle about the fucking and sucking of children, and then watch Angelina Jolie promote her latest adoption. Ah, entertainment.

Children get fucked and sucked and killed. For no reason, they suffer and die. The priests aren't punished. Michael Jackson isn't punished. The military isn't punished. Al-Qaeda isn't punished. Only the guilty, it seems, are allowed to remain innocent.

Unless you're this guy: A former Natick High School teacher and coach was sentenced to prison yesterday after admitting he used the internet to lure an undercover detective, posing as a 14-year-old boy, for sex. I didn't hear any jokes about *him* on the television last night. Too bad, because I think that's fucking hilarious.

Here's what he had to say when he addressed the court: "As an educator and someone who cared very much about his students and players, I should have seen what I was doing was wrong. I beg Your Honor for leniency." He received a sentence of up to five years in prison for his honesty.

So maybe the lesson to be learned is to never admit you did anything wrong.

Which may not make any sense, but then nothing makes much sense around here these days. When simple ideas like 'destroying children is wrong' can somehow become thorny issues of debate, I no longer believe there is any such thing as heroes and all of us are guilty.

Dear Al-Qaeda.

There is loose change scattered all over our kitchen floor, in various displays of heads & tails. One coin's president is afraid to show his face in the darker places. Outside, earlier, I walked around the wet cement signs that block our sidewalk.

A lawnmower across the street is leaking gas. It burns holes in the asphalt, which burns through the asphalt into the soil, and then burns a path straight through to China like the one we tried to dig when we were younger only to end up ankle-deep in all that water. So we made mud pies and mud pastries, mud disguises and mud disgrace, all over the daughter of the babysitter's face. I licked it off, and though I washed my tongue several times that night, it still remained gray.

Maya cried today because she never wants to get old, and though there is much to be unsure about lately on the subject of Scott & Maya Inc., I can be certain that she will. She will grow old. She will sag in all the saggier places. Children will play connect-the-dots with her liver spots. I don't even know where liver spots come from, or calcium deposits for that matter.

Are calcium deposits caused by too much calcium in your diet? Are liver spots the result of too much liver? Too much living? Is cellulite merely an abundance of cells?

I do not know, but I know that you will sag and droop my darling. Your tits will chase the floor like your frown. They droop even now, when I turn you upside down in ever-shortening breaths.

Dear Al-Qaeda.

And when you enter, her ellipse will become a circle.

Dear Al-Qaeda.

It is my understanding that you do not work, that you do not spend your days and nights at a job in order to survive, in order to do what we call 'making a living.' I have heard that you are supported by wealthy Arab *mullahs* who agree with your cause and send you all the money you need, whenever you need it, to help you fulfill your goals.

I want a cause, Al-Qaeda. And now, as I rapidly approach my 33rd birthday, I can say that I'm becoming less choosy about which causes I'm willing to embrace. It seems unfair to me that you should spend your days planning terrorist attacks with no worry where the next dollar will come from, while I am forced to write these letters, and other more literary pursuits, in stolen days off from my job, in the process neglecting my girlfriend and even, on occasion, our cat. I would like to say this is your fault, Al-Qaeda. It would help me sleep easier at night to say so. But I'm starting to believe the fault lies within our own society. Within–if such a thing is possible–America itself.

Don't misunderstand. I am not willing to join you. I have no wish to hurt anyone, let alone kill them, let alone destroy their way of life.

But I am tired Al-Qaeda, very tired indeed.

Dear Al-Qaeda.

I've been doing some thinking, and it occurs to me that we have another thing in common. We both have this vision of utopia, and we're pissed that the human race keeps falling short of our ideals. Granted, we have chosen different methods of trying to convince people. You fly planes into buildings and kill thousands of people; I write poetry.

Yeah. Poetry.

It was either that or become a plumber, and looking back, I should've gone into plumbing. I mean, have you watched Judge Judy lately? Plumbers all over the place. Yet we haven't allowed a poet on television since The Steve Allen Show back in the 1950's, and even then Steve insisted on playing the piano while Jack Kerouac read.

Actually, I did read poetry on tv once, but it was on this public access show in Prescott, Arizona, where the host–a lady named Lady–was dressed like a Keebler elf. I sat in one chair, and the lady–I mean *Lady*, sat in the other. Between us stood a water fountain, with water trickling down some fake rocks as Lady asked me when I first knew I wanted to be a writer. Between questions, I read some of my poems.

This must sound weird even to you, Al-Qaeda. You're probably thinking to yourself: Why does he write poetry? Nobody writes poetry.

Well I don't anymore. The only thing I write now is letters to you. No more abstract images meant to trigger a reaction in the reader's subconscious. We are living in fucked-up times, Al-Qaeda. No point in hiding behind metaphors now.

Too bad, I was a really good poet, too.

Dear Al-Qaeda.

You probably call it rock and roll, or maybe the devil's music like people used to do all those years ago. I doubt you call it nigger music, though people used to call it that too. This genre called rock and roll contains several hundred variations and subgenres underneath its umbrella. They differ in sound, from clean to distorted, from passive to intense, from light to dark.

One of the darkest of all rock and roll genres, the most distorted, the most intense, is something called death metal. In death metal, the drums hammer and pound, the guitars grind and sludge, the band throws their hair around in simultaneous circles like some kind of follicle color guard, and then there's a singer.

Death metal singers growl in these absurdly deep voices. They're meant to sound scary, because the world is a scary place or something. You know how in monster movies, when the monster jumps out from behind a bush and makes the girl scream, and he makes this sound like *bwaaarrrr!*?

Death metal singers sound like that.

They think they sound like dangerous caged tigers, when they're really just a kittycat who doesn't want to get off the sofa.

There's a concert coming up November 23rd at the Masquerade in Ybor City. A festival of death metal bands:

Cannibal Corpse
Napalm Death
Goatwhore
Kataklysm
Vada

I am not making this up. Do you know what these big scary people do at their concerts, Al-Qaeda? With names like Cannibal Corpse, I'm sure you're imagining that it must be far deadlier than anything a group like the gentle sounding Al-Qaeda could ever imagine.

Let me tell you what these big scary men do. They plug their amplifiers into electrical outlets. Then they plug their guitars, which are made of wood and wire, into these amplifiers. Then they hold a piece of plastic between their thumb and forefinger, and pluck those strings while making that aforementioned growling sound into a microphone. Then, after sixty minutes or so, they stop.

Afterwards, they hang out backstage and fuck self-hating underage girls. Or get back on their bus, which was paid for by the record company, the company they work for.

Now, I'll grant you, they pluck those strings pretty goddamn hard. But enough to justify a name like Napalm Death? Al-Qaeda, these men have never killed anyone. Cannibal Corpse has never eaten another human being. I doubt they've even seen a cannibal; and aside from a grandmother's funeral, I doubt they've ever seen a corpse. And they, the band, are certainly not corpses. I know this for a fact because the ad says "LIVE" in big letters right underneath their name.

For that matter, Napalm Death has never seen napalm. They are, I assume, also not dead. Goatwhore are not goats, nor do they own them. They are also not whores. In fact, I would guess that seeing Julia Roberts in *Pretty Woman* is probably the closest they've ever been to a whore.

Cataclysm? (For let's spell it correctly. These men are too scary to even spell correctly, Al-Qaeda. *Spelling is for pussies! We spit blood on your linguistic conventions!*) Doesn't a name like Cataclysm imply, oh, I don't know, something cataclysmic? Like an ending? But no, these guys are playing plenty more shows on this tour, nothing cataclysmic about that.

I have no idea what Vada means, though I imagine it's supposed to frighten me.

The point I'm taking my sweet-ass time in getting to, Al-Qaeda, is who do these fucking guys think they are, in the wake of September 11th, to try and pass themselves off as scary? Let's compare growing pubic hair on your face and not bathing to hijacking a plane with a boxcutter and fly-ing it into a fucking skyscraper. I don't think these guys are that tough. In fact, I can't see how they're able to keep a straight face. One would think that September 11th would have rendered the whole "scary musician" thing null and void, about as socially relevant as Pat Boone in a cardigan. But still they soldier on, Al-Qaeda. And if I were you, I'd be even more pissed off than you normally are. Here, Al-Qaeda goes travelling the earth and killing inno-cent people, while these guys travel the earth entertaining them, and yet somehow *they're* supposed to be the badasses? Make an example of them, Al-Qaeda. The Masquerade holds a couple thousand people, but I doubt anyone will mourn the innocent deaths. Two thousand less telemarketers and 7-11 clerks. You'd be doing everyone a favor, including the audience.

You could do this in your sleep. No plane necessary. Show

them who the real badasses are.

November 23rd. The Masquerade. Ybor City.

Let's call it a date.

Dear Al-Qaeda.

People are bored; they are not free. They do not know how to say so.

Given the choice, they would say so.

Dear Al-Qaeda.

Evil can be anywhere. It lurks in corners behind a saintly mask where the Easter Bunny eats children while Santa bribes senators, the razor blade in the candy apple and who really cares if the sun rises twenty years from now or if the earth continues to warm.

A toothless minister on a gloomy *Parade* magazine Sunday, sanitized and scrubbed clean to perfection, will insist that he knows the truth. But who's to say that heaven isn't evil, that our Christian God isn't actually an imposter and that our suffering is only an illusion.

When reasonable people insist that drinking your own urine is nutritious and plastic surgery is good for your soul, that protein will kill you and carbohydrates are stealing our youth as rivers run backwards and rainwater causes cancer, then what kind of fool believes we ever went to the moon. Didn't you see the shadows? Every water moccasin has two heads and a vanishing tail; they make great house-pets if they don't strangle your children first. Super Bowl Sunday is the most popular day of the year for domestic abuse except that it's not. The internet tells me all of these ideas are true, and that nobody reads the newspaper anymore because the newspapers have too liberal a bias. Unless, that is, you believe they are too conservative because they are all owned by corporations. You see, it all depends on the telling and only a trusting fool would trust the truth any further than the last hastily written paragraph.

Though faith at least provides a paycheck, assuming you're the type of person who can still be consoled.

Dear Al-Qaeda.

There's this holiday called Thanksgiving, I believe we celebrate it on the third Thursday of November. On this day, we eat turkey in honor of the pilgrims who landed on this continent in 1620, and the Native Americans who helped teach these newcomers how to survive the harsh New England winter. We hang pictures of people with belt buckles on their hats, eat way too much food, and then watch the Detroit Lions lose a football game, all while trying to ignore the fact that our ancestors ended up slaughtering the generous Native Americans. It's a lot of fun.

When I was little, I would wake up on Thanksgiving morning and rush to the tv in order to watch the Macy's Thanksgiving Day Parade. Scores of floats and balloons would make their way down New York City, and at the end of the parade Santa Claus would appear to announce the beginning of Christmas. It was all very exciting, especially when the Charlie Brown and Underdog balloons showed up. I loved Underdog when I was three.

Anyway, I woke up early this Thanksgiving, and while flipping the channels I decided to watch some of the parade. An attempt to recapture the innocence of my childhood, or maybe because I live in Florida now and the 80 degree sunshine on Thanksgiving morning sent me scrambling for tradition.

Al-Qaeda, the parade was a big pile of bullshit. The floats were one long procession of commercials and mediocrity. Watching the tv hosts–on NBC: Matt Lauer, Katie Couric, and Al Roeker–gush at the Hess float, it took a strong man to watch without laughing, or throwing up.

Hess is an oil company, so maybe you've heard of them. They own gas stations. The Hess float, charmingly titled "Hess Corporation's Bridge to the Future Float," was 32 feet long, 20 feet wide, and 30 feet tall, and incorporated an elevated highway which spanned a modernized reproduction of New York City's Brooklyn Bridge to the Delta Y Suspension Bridge of Tomorrow. Despite my best attempts at research, I have no idea where the latter bridge is, or when the bridge's "tomorrow" may become "today."

The float also featured a large-scale Hess Toy Truck–this toy truck is celebrating its 40th anniversary and I didn't even know it existed–a Hess SUV towing two Hess motorcycles, a Hess Toy Truck shuttle, and a replica of Hess' first truck.

There's your commercial, now for the mediocrity. The Hess float featured a relatively unknown singer named Gavin DeGraw, performing "I Don't Want To Be" a song off his new album *Chariot*. Despite the album's title, Gavin looked less like a Roman emperor than an Abercrombie model. As for the song itself, allow me to quote some lyrics:

Can I have everyone's attention please?

All I have to do is think of me and I have peace of mind.

If you're not like this and that,
you're gonna have to leave.

I came from the mountain, the coast of creation.

A mix of egomania & idiocy, if you ask me. Anyway, this all leads up to the chorus, which goes like this:

I don't want to be anything
other than what I've been trying to be lately.

Go back and read that again, Al-Qaeda: *I don't want to be anything other than what I've been trying to be lately.* Not since a group called America (they won a Grammy Award back in the seventies for Best New Artist–please also bomb the Grammys, Al-Qaeda) sang, "Oz never did give nothing to the Tin Man that he didn't didn't already have," has such a vague and grammatically-confused song come strolling down the pike.

You should have seen Gavin, Al-Qaeda, strutting around the float in his faded hundred dollar jeans. In the face of it all, I felt compelled to do a little research. Apparently, Gavin attended the Berklee school of music in Boston. Not to be confused with the differently-spelled, more radical namesake in California, Berklee is a school for rich kids to practice being rockstar American Idol-type performers, complete with classes on how to hold the microphone and learning where to put your hands while standing on stage. Because, you know, that's what all the great musicians did. Take a college class in stagecraft.

These little music fuckers are responsible for eliminating the best cheap lunch in Boston. This bar called Bukowski's used to feature a dollar burger special, which they had to discontinue thanks to the Berklee kids who would come in there with their Banana Republic pants and Armani sweaters, and proceed to order a couple of burgers and water instead of the delicious beer served at this *bar*, thus violating the unspoken agreement existing between Bukowski's and their customers: that we don't try to rip them off and fuck up a good deal. But they did.

Thanks a lot Gavin DeGraw. Thank you.

Getting back to the float. Hess also had a bunch of kids dressed up as traffic signs, with their little ten-year-old heads poking out of signs reading YIELD, STOP, and the like. The kids bopped along behind Gavin as he reached down into the shallows of his artistic soul and belted his song–this celebration of not wanting to be anything other than what he's been trying to be lately. That is, a star.

As the song wore on, I found myself noticing that only certain kids could be seen in the close-ups standing behind Gavin, which made me wonder who decided which kids would get to be seen on tv. Did Hess choose the most photogenic? Or did the biggest kids just elbow the others out of the way? Or maybe an overbearing stage-mother threw a shit fit until Tommy got the spot behind Gavin, hoping against hope that some commercial producer would see her beautiful smiling little cabbage and decide to use him to hock some sugar-damaged breakfast cereal.

We are now a long way from turkey, family, and Native Americans.

Oh Al-Qaeda, when you struck New York City–when you brought that city to its collective knees–who could have imagined that in the wake of all that destruction New York City would rise from the ashes of 9/11, would somehow persevere, just so some talentless histrionic dickface could sing down its streets even as American soldiers died that very morning in Iraq? Who could have imagined all these soldiers dying in order to help him achieve peace of mind, when all he really needed to do for peace of mind was think of himself?

Come back to New York, Al-Qaeda. It's so beautiful in the fall with the leaves turning color and everything. By the way, Katie Couric loved Gavin DeGraw. I swear she actually gushed, which either makes her a liar or a fool and to be honest, I'm tired of trying to make up my mind.

Dear Al-Qaeda.

I have not cleaned the apartment in over a week. There is dust all over the television, on top of the television, on the screen, in the screen, in the pictures on the screen. Dust on the tv; dust in the tv. I shake the tv and dust falls like in a snowglobe. It collects in Tony Danza's hair, and when you shake the tv some more, the dust falls onto the collar of his navy sportcoat like dandruff or actual snow. The channel makes no difference. A different tv personality, a different blazer, but we are all made of dust and the television won't stop shaking.

Dear Al-Qaeda.

I thought they didn't exist anymore. I had assumed they were relics from a bygone age.

Even that word–debutante–it just seemed like so much black & white tv.

I should capitalize debutante. So it looks like this, "Debutante." Because that's how they wrote it on the invitation. Come to think of it, I'll show you the invitation ...

The Parents of the Debutantes

of

Two thousand and four

request the pleasure of your company

at the

Presentation Ball and Reception

Tuesday, the twenty-eighth of December

eight o'clock

The Coliseum

Saint Petersburg, Florida

~ Black Tie ~

Seating at half past seven o'clock

Listed inside are the names of the proud "Parents of the Debutantes," followed by a list of the twenty Debutantes, arranged in alphabetical order, presumably to prevent cat-fights.

The Coliseum bills itself as "The Finest Climate-Controlled Ballroom in Florida," and who's going to argue with them? Certainly not me. But then I consider a building shaped like an airplane hangar and painted the pink color of raw salmon and the aqua-green of the Miami Dolphins' jerseys to be quite "fine" indeed. Picture yourself watching tv in 1984, picture the word "Miami," then picture the word "Vice." Now see the color of each word. Now imagine your television is the size of an airplane hangar. Welcome to The Coliseum, which is not a coliseum at all, but a ballroom. A climate-controlled ballroom.

There is a stage at the far end of The Coliseum. The walls jut out around the stage to form the shape of a castle. This castle is the aforementioned color of pink, with the words "The Coliseum" written on the top of the castle in that aforementioned aqua-green. Eight Greek columns spread across the stage, each rising ten feet into the air, with bouquets of roses rising out of the top of each column. This was meant to represent . . . actually, I have nothing. I have no idea. Greek fucking columns. Placed around the stage. For a debutante ball. With roses sticking out of the top. I guess eleven models of the Eiffel Tower with ivy weaving in and out of the girders just seemed ridiculous.

As we started to set up for the party, throw tablecloths over the tables, the Debutantes began to file in with their mothers. Apparently a Debutante is someone who works at Abercrombie & Fitch. Do you wear flip-flops with jeans? You too may be a Debutante. Especially if your name is Chelsea Elizabeth Silverstein, the daughter of Mr.

and Mrs. Murray Bruce Silverstein. Or if your name is Andrea Claire Boulay, daughter of Dr. and Mrs. Joseph Alfred Boulay, Junior.

Do you see Swedish meatballs everyday? You too may be a caterer. Especially if you see cubes of cheese stacked on a tray to form an even larger cube, or crackers from a box fanned out along the bottom of the tray, or sushi purchased from the local grocery store, and egg rolls sliced in half at the owner's insistence because they'll "go further." Only the best for the lovely ladies of St. Petersburg.

The ball began a couple of hours later, and the Debutantes reappeared transformed, like Cinderella, from typical Florida beachgoers into princesses, complete with white dresses and tiaras. The Debutantes were introduced one at a time along with their presenters. In most cases, this duty was fulfilled by their fathers. In the case of a broken home, however, they were presented by the man who had taken their father's place.

The father, or "father," presented his Debutante by walking arm and arm with her around a half-circle of twenty escorts–the male version of a Debutante. I assume it was worked out in advance who would escort each Debutante, because after completing their presentation, each Debutante walked over to her escort and dropped to one knee. At first, I thought she might start sucking his dick, but alas and alack, she just got back up to her feet and shared a dance with her escort.

This went on, one Debutante at a time, for about two hours. After all of the Debutantes had been presented, escorted, and danced, everyone in the audience got up and joined them; the mothers, friends, relatives, etc. Not the caterers though. We sat there bored and yawning, waiting for them to finish so we could clean up their shit and go home. I can't even ask you to harm them, Al-Qaeda, such is my boredom. I've been home for three hours now, and it shows no sign of stopping, especially with Maya already in bed without so much as bothering to say goodnight to me. For we are both bored, and in our boredom it won't be long before we start to devour each other simply for the sake of something to do.

We just don't fit in, being in Florida. Everybody here is waiting to die; we seem to be the only ones waiting to live.

Dear Al-Qaeda.

This is what passes for thought when I can't decide whether to close the windows.

We surround ourselves with beauty but it makes no difference. We cover our walls with posters, with cheesy thrift store paintings of baby ducks, or fine art, or Jesus, or cuttings from the Weekly World News. And given time all the words and images fade at last into facts, and we walk past them without seeing, already disgruntled, wondering why our homes are dull and uninspiring. This fading, the inevitable fading.

In my experience, this process takes about three months.

I believe our society measures the degree of one's sanity, one's ability to conform, by one's indifference to all this fading. To shrug your shoulders is the greatest sign of respect you can pay to a building, or a spouse.

*****

She tears through her various fragrances like a chainsaw through a spice rack. Candles and lotions, body sprays and shampoos. Around every corner a new scent, a new way to color the world, and maybe this scent will be the one to last, to not fade.

This is as close to prayer as she allows.

*****

If I ever get to dedicate something to my girlfriend, I want to have the kind of relationship that would enable me to put the words "long-suffering" immediately before her name. Because I'd rather atone for my failings all at once than spend the better part of my days apologizing, taking the other person's feelings into consideration. Hell, that alone is reason enough to be a writer. Bartenders don't get to dedicate their drinks, fast-food hamburgers have no meaning, a president never puts a name on his bombs. Dedications are a perk of the business, as the saying goes.

And while we're on the topic of sayings, I'll end with some wisdom from Maya's mother.

If wishes and buts were candy and nuts, we'd all have a Merry Christmas.

I wish we weren't like this and I don't know how to make it stop.

Dear Al-Qaeda.

Did you know the catering business experiences a lull each January? Neither did we. So Maya and I got jobs at this place called RGIS until business picks up again.

RGIS stands for Retail Grocery Inventory Specialists, and is always pronounced "Are-Gee-Eye-Ess." It is never, ever pronounced "regis," presumably due to legal issues between them and the hair salon in Tyrone Plaza, if not Regis Philbin.

So we are auditors. That is our official title, in case you're wondering. An auditor goes to various stores–K-Mart, Michael's, Publix, etc.–and inventories the store. And by "inventory," I mean point a laser gun at a barcode and squeeze the trigger. The audit machine then produces a loud BEEP. You scan each item in your area and write the total count on an area ticket. In most stores you average between 400 and 600 BEEPs per hour. The inventory lasts until all the areas have been audited, typically anywhere from three to five hours.

Let me tell you about our co-workers. They are haggard, Al-Qaeda, and after a couple of weeks, we are already haggard as well. Most stores don't want a lot of BEEPing going on while they're open, so we either have to go in before the store opens, or after they close. This means a typical workday involves showing up at 5am, doing an inventory, then coming home and going back to a different store at 6pm. We have replaced a good night's sleep with a bad afternoon's nap. I feel like I'm back in college again, pounding coffee through the day to compensate for my four hours of sleep from the night before, though this is an education I'd prefer not to be getting.

The other night we inventoried a Steinmart, which is like a T.J. Maxx for people who either have too much money or too many liver spots. I don't know if Steinmart is actually owned by Germans, but it certainly had a German-like efficiency when it came to annoying the fuck out of me. Understand, the worst part of this job is the piped-in music playing in the stores. You think it's bad hearing that bullshit when you're shopping, try hearing it for five hours, accompanied by a loud BEEP every few seconds. And Steinmart had the worst music I've heard so far. It sounded like Kenny G if he lost his edge, or like taking three percocets and getting a blowjob from Betty White on the Golden Girls' wicker sofa.

The RGIS boss placed me in accessories. My area was this spinning rack filled with earrings, and the barcode I needed to scan was on the back of these earrings. So I had to lift each earring up in order to get at the barcode, but because they were so packed together, I would knock two or three off every time I tried. I spent three hours in this particular circle of hell and ended up breaking several pairs of earrings, some of them by accident.

I want to quit, Al-Qaeda. Even as I write this, we have to wake up in three hours to go do a Publix. It's a grocery store. Maya's mom calls it "pube-licks." Last night, we were at a Hollister, which is an Abercrombie & Fitch for people who wished they lived in California, until two in the morning because this particular Hollister had already gotten in their summer line–six months early. Their back-room was packed to the ceiling with boxes. It is January; nobody expected this. Needless to say, this slowed our BEEP time considerably. Hearing her sob into her pillow as she fell asleep, I think Maya may have already given up.

We learned an interesting fact about Hollister tonight. You know all the beautiful teenagers they have working there? Well they don't do a whole hell of a lot of work. Once the store closes, Hollister has all these Mexicans come in and do all the stocking and refolding, as well as the nightly cleaning duties. It turns out the daytime employees, the upscale blonde children of America, don't just *appear* to spend all of their time dicking around on the floor and occasionally running the cash register. That is all they do. What's more, each employee not only has to wear Hollister clothing at all times, *including their shoes*– which in this case were flip-flops–but they have to be wearing the clothes which belong to that particular season. This was not the case for the Mexican workers, apparently, who were wearing that season's line from Goodwill.

Hollister has nearly forty employees, not counting the after-hours Hispanic help, and considering that each employee works no more than twenty hours a week, one wonders how they are able to survive, let alone afford Hollister's clothes, even at an employee discount. Oh yeah, their parents are rich. So not only does Hollister pay next to nothing for labor, but most of their clothes feature the word HOLLISTER in big letters across the front. So advertising costs must be low, since the clothes advertise themselves and all. And don't even ask me where the clothes were manufactured.

Not that I care, not that anyone cares beyond the self-righteous feeling they get from not shopping at stores like Hollister, or in malls like International Plaza. They believe they are superior to most people because they don't shop at the mall. So what. They're not smart enough to realize that they already live in one.

From the apartment complex where we swim in a pool to the restaurant with an apostrophe in its name where we go to unwind, this whole country is a mall. When the only reason we exist is to spend our money, and American culture only exists to take it, there can be no other explanation.

I cannot quit my job at RGIS because I need money, not to buy a new pair of jeans, but simply to buy our freedom. This job is not fun. Everyone who works here has a face like a cigarette and a tongue like black coffee. In two weeks, I have yet to hear a funny joke. There's this one old guy who sounds like a cross between Michael McDonald's singing voice and Hank Hill. I call him Hank McDonald. I understand this name isn't funny. I mention it to show you that the quiet death of my co-workers, their beaten-down-by-their-own-lives-ness has already begun to infect me. Maya & I don't want to quit. The only reason we're still living in this penis-shaped state is so we can save enough money to get the hell out, but at what expense, Al-Qaeda? At the expense of our very souls? Of our goddamned personalities?

Fuck this. I will quit. I am quitting. If I don't quit now, there won't be any Scott left to enjoy this life I'm working to create. I'm not even going to give them notice. And why should I? Every job I've ever been fired from, or had my hours reduced, they never gave me any notice. And besides, Florida is a right-to-work state. That nice sounding phrase–"right-to-work"–essentially means that any employer can fire me at any time for any reason with no notice or warning whatsoever. So, as a Florida resident, I will invoke my "right-to-work" and choose not to. No more BEEP.

Dear Al-Qaeda.

Do you ever wish you were more beautiful? I don't know what passes for beauty where you live, but it seems that in America we prefer our women to have blonde hair, sharp noses, even sharper breasts, and the hollowed-out cheekbones that can only come from a lifetime of cocaine abuse.

Allow me to digress. There's this television show on Fox called "The Swan," which involves two women who are chosen to compete in a beauty contest. The winner of each show moves on to the final round, a glorious twelve-woman competition to decide who will become America's Swan.

The twist? The show's producers choose the ugliest, women possible, either on the outside or the inside, it makes no difference, though both are preferable. Say an overweight mother of three whose mother locked her in a closet when she was young. Or a sergeant in the army whose stepdad fondled her breasts. Apparently, knocking your teeth out with a hammer will increase your chances of appearing on the show as well.

The two contestants are then sent to Swan Camp, where they're given access to the finest plastic surgeons in the world. They participate in therapy and physical fitness programs as well, though this seems to be done more to convince the Swans they are earning their new beauty; the surgery will be so dramatic that it will make situps redundant. All fat is liposuctioned. All teeth are replaced. Hair is extended. And of course breasts are sculpted to D-cup perfection.

The women are not allowed to see themselves in a mirror while at Swan Camp. Each episode makes a point to show Swan security going through the women's belongings when they arrive at Swan Camp and confiscating all reflective surfaces. Though anyone who has ever turned on a lamp at night and stood in front of a window can tell you there are other ways to see your reflection.

Three months in Swan Camp gets reduced to 40 minutes on tv, minus commercials. Each Swan cries when she realizes the experience is more difficult than she first assumed, that plastic surgery is painful, and that as a mother, she actually misses her children when separated from them for three months. Finally at the end of the show, after the bruises have faded and their broken bones have healed, the Swans are dressed in expensive clothes and led to the show's climax.

They are brought into an enormous, extravagantly furnished foyer, where their plastic surgeons, therapists, coaches, etc. are all gathered to applaud the Swan as she enters the room. In one corner stands a curtain that stretches from ceiling to floor. Behind this curtain is a mirror, but before the Swan can see herself she must first be revealed to the audience.

The Swan, in every case, is unrecognizable as the person who arrived in Swan Camp. Still, she does look familiar. Oh yeah. She looks like all the Swans from every episode. Instead of making these women into more beautiful versions of themselves, the doctors instead have chosen to sculpt them into an early 21st century standard of beauty because . . . you know . . . you might as well–as long as you're there with the knife and all.

The Swan stands before the curtain, which is pulled aside with a dramatic flourish. She sees herself in the mirror for the first time, and every Swan has the same reaction. She screams. Then she slaps her hands to her face like Macaulay Culkin in *Home Alone* and screams some more, with pleasure. Then she squeals, "It doesn't even look like me!" or something along those lines. This idea, that she no longer looks like herself, that pictures from her childhood will no longer bear any resemblance to this person in the mirror, fills her with pleasure. And since she came onto the show already hating herself, why wouldn't it?

The second Swan comes out, and the process is repeated. Then comes the show's sickest twist. The two Swans stand next to each other as the show's judges determine who will advance to the final Swan Pageant, meaning one of these women–who has just been made "beautiful"–*will now be told thirty seconds later that she is not beautiful enough.*

A winner is chosen to move on, a loser is left behind. The show ends. Credits roll. We are given a preview of next week's Swans, of their ugly tragic lives and the promise that their suffering is about to end.

I don't tell you this for any reason, Al-Qaeda, other than to blow your mind at how we choose to live and what we consider entertainment. Please do not terrorize any Swans. They are probably already dying, even as I write this. Besides, Maya and I watch the show every week. I'd go so far as to say we watch it religiously, if I didn't think you might take it the wrong way.

Dear Al-Qaeda.

Last Sunday was Super Bowl Sunday, one of the more religious of our non-religious holidays. And as Madonna once sang, "Holiday. Celebrate." And so a bunch of restaurant workers in the St. Pete area decided to do their celebrating at Orange Blossom.

Not to get all Jeff Foxworthy here, but if you bring your own beer cozy to a catered party . . . you *might* be a redneck. If you bring your own inflatable Bud Light thunderstick and then proceed to beat my girlfriend with it, then you're probably an asshole *and* a redneck.

The leader of this group of restaurants, the man who put the party together, was this fat, Jabba The Hut-type lizard named Sly, who insisted on being given a microphone and p.a., only to use said microphone to shout at people for the duration of the Super Bowl. For the occasion, Sly rented fifteen 24-inch televisions to be placed at random tables, when really 4 big-screens would have done the job.

The pre-game festivities involved door prizes and prayer, two of our country's favorite pastimes. The stack of 200 lottery tickets was won by this guy with a blonde perm and six pelicans encircling his dress shirt. His name, it turned out, was B.J. The woman who won a coupon book good for 25 free pizzas from an Italian restaurant wore an oversized t-shirt that looked like a screensaver from 1993, along with matching sweatpants. She wore sandals. Everyone wore sandals. I imagined the callouses that must form between your toes after a lifetime of sandals. I wondered if you could shove a thumbtack into one of these callouses, or if it would just snap off and break in the attempt.

With the door prizes out of the way, it was time to take, in Sly's words, "a moment of silence for our boys trying to save freedom around the world." Heads were dutifully bowed.

A few minutes later, the fifteen televisions began our National Anthem, and everyone stood up. The man closest to me, with the shaved head and the moustache, had a beer cozy that read, *Capt. Hook's Mulletwear: Our Drinking Team Has A Fishing Problem*. He placed his right hand over his heart, or tried to; I doubt his heart is located in his left shoulder. He looked like he was about to be wrapped in a straitjacket; as the evening progressed I began to feel like joining him.

In addition to the swedish meatballs and baked potatoes, the Orange Blossom chefs prepared a lovely cheese spread which, thanks to the magic of food coloring, was an exact replica of the Super Bowl football field, right down to the Patriots and Eagles logos in each end zone. This cheese spread led to a weird exchange when I joked to one of the guests that it was the first time I'd ever intentionally eaten green cheese. She replied, "I didn't even know it was a football field at first!" I'm not sure what she thought it was, considering you have to cut the cheese out of the field in order to eat it. And the cheese was green. With white hashmarks. Sure.

Nick spent the evening slipping beers into his apron and bringing them out behind Orange Blossom for us to drink as quickly as possible. And yes, the party's "bar" consisted of coolers filled with cans of beer and bags of ice. After the seventh or so apron smuggle, the football game ceased to exist. The event became paper plates that needed to be transferred from a table to a trashcan as we walked from the back alley to the cooler. Even Maya drank a little.

The evening progressed. Ignorance became slurred ignorance, Sly got a little fatter, we all got a lot drunker, the sun went down, and I hear the Patriots won. Each caterer took home over sixty dollars in tips, and who cares about the people who got into their cars when they could barely get into a bathroom. I mean, this is a holiday after all.

Dear Al-Qaeda.

We were at Wal-Mart today because we needed some cat food–god knows there's nothing else to do here in central Florida–when I came up with this great idea for a game show. Maya was unimpressed, so I'm hoping you'll be a more receptive audience.

Every time we go there, I see all these fat people rolling around Wal-Mart in their motorized wheelchairs. But I don't think they're handicapped at all. Judging by the unbaked Pillsbury dough of their asses, I think that they're just too fat and lazy to walk. Each ass hangs over the seat of its wheelchair until it obscures the seat from view–like the swollen ankle that folds over itself several times until it becomes multiple ankles and then droops over the top of each sneaker.

On my game show, the contestants will guess whether or not these people need their wheelchair. I will call it, *Crippled or Obese?*

So on the game show a Wal-Mart shopper will wheel themselves onto the stage, where three contestants will guess whether they are *crippled*, that is to say: authentically handicapped, or just so obese and/or lazy that they use a Wal-Mart scooter to get around the store–clogging up the aisles like cat hair in a Liquid Plumber commercial, or like a piece of shit that got caught in my throat.

After the contestants have written down their answers, the wheelchair-person will attempt to stand up and walk. Imagine the suspense as they teeter back and forth, all the while their girth shaking. Crippled? Obese? Maybe we'll put a corndog on the other side of the stage as some kind of incentive. Imagine the audience's gasps as the Cripples fall to the ground in agony. Imagine their surprise, and subsequent cheers, as the Obese lumber across the stage towards their compensatory corndog. This is good stuff, Al-Qaeda. The prize, of course, would be Wal-Mart shopping cards–which save you 3-cents a gallon at the Wal-Mart gas pumps, and Allah knows with the price of gas going through the fucking ceiling . . .

Wal-Mart could sponsor the show. Their business would soar, I imagine, with so many Obesities and/or Cripples heading there to practice, to surround themselves with as many motorized-wheelchair people as possible, so they might not embarrass themselves on national tv.

Because if there's one thing we hate, as Americans, it is to be embarrassed on national tv.

Dear Al-Qaeda.

Orange Blossom just catered this event in Sun City. Located about thirty miles south from St. Petersburg, Sun City is a retirement community for seniors. Last Friday, they had a formal winter gala, which I like to call a "Senior Prom," though my Senior Prom didn't have an open bar.

You walk into the ballroom, flanked on both sides by eight-foot Roman columns which Maya insists I describe as "insidious & hollow." Here's a line from my notes:

The fur coats in florida spend their whole lives waiting for this, dancing how glorious they must have imagined.

I have to admit that Maya's is better, but I need to mention the fur coats, which were draped on every other chair. It was 75 degrees out. Fahrenheit. Not exactly fur weather.

But then why wouldn't you wear fur? After all, judging by the February events calendar, this was definitely a big night out for the Sun Citizens. In case any of you guys are stocking money into your 401K–or 401Q being Arabic and all–and dream of retiring to Florida to live the good life, here's what you can look forward to for entertainment.

> **Saturday, Feb. 5th.** *"Party Mardi Gras Style." Music provided by Court Jester Bryan Ashley. Features a "Ragin' Cajun Menu," which includes Tossed Salad Family Style, Roast Pork Loin, and Bread Pudding w/ Bourbon Sauce. The cost is $15.00.*

Saturday, Feb. 19th. *"Magic of Malaysia." A photo presentation by digital photographer Jim Peterson of the "delightful southeast Asian nation." $7.00. Food will not be served.*

Which is too bad. I was looking forward to the "Ragin' Malaysian menu."

Wednesday, Feb. 23rd. *"Hobo Nite / Line Dance." There will be a prize for best hobo attire. $5.50.*

Also, an important notice:

The Cracker Barrel Trip *has been moved from Feb. 28th to Mar. 1st because the Cracker Barrel isn't open on Mondays.*

And to prove that irony still exists, even in Sun City, "Yesterday" was playing over the muzak in the hall as I wrote all of this down.

While clearing some plates from one of the tables, the owner of one of those fur coats tried to get my attention by actually tugging on the back of my jacket like she was pulling a paper towel from the bathroom dispenser. When I turned around, she said, "I need you to bring me some coffee." I told her she needed to stop pulling on my jacket and walked away. If I have learned one thing in my months of catering, it's that you need to be firm with the guests. You at least need to be firmer than the loose skin on that woman's finger, jammed through a diamond ring and dangling from the bottom of a bird-like claw.

But please do not bomb them, Al-Qaeda. They already have so little to live for and you are not known for your mercy.

Dear Al-Qaeda.

I knew nothing about drag racing before this weekend. I knew the cars go really fast, and there's a parachute at the end. That was about it.

Having spent the last four days catering an NHRA championship drag racing event–bringing food in and out of the luxury suites where fans watch the races–I have learned more than I ever wanted to know. I am not talking about the rednecks. I have seen plenty of t-shirts like WIFE FOR SALE: CHEAP in my lifetime. I have seen enough mullets and stretchpants and the rest. I grew up near Cajon Speedway, which bills itself as "the fastest 3/8 mile paved oval in the west," in El Cajon, California. After high school, I worked for a couple of years at an amusement park called Marshal Scotty's, which had a go-cart track where the Cajon Speedway drivers would go to unwind.

I know what a man's hands look like when he spends his free time devoted to his car.

However, I did not know why people attend drag racing events. Now I know. They attend them in the hope of getting cancer, apparently. The big cars, I forget what they're called, run on nitromethane. Basically, it sets off an explosion in the engine which shoots the car down the track at speeds in excess of 280 miles per hour with a force nearly five times that of gravity, the same force aboard the Space Shuttle when it takes off from Cape Canaveral. The sound it makes is fucking loud. I can't write BOOM in a big enough font. It sounded like a bomb, or a plane flying into a building.

All of this is interesting, but not nearly as interesting as the cloud of nitrous that drifts over the bleachers after the cars have taken off.

The gasoline fumes can cause cancer. If you're exposed to them for prolonged periods, a rash will break out all over your arm and you will feel a burning sensation. A prolonged period, in this case, being a couple of hours. Each night, the direction of the wind would push the nitrous clouds straight through the bleachers to our right. Parents, fearing for their young children's safety, had been sure to bring earplugs to protect them from the BOOM, but didn't bother to cover their children's skin.

Now I don't know the exact science of all this, because most of my information is second-hand, from other people working the event. The caterers had been provided a luxury suite so we wouldn't have to spend the whole day outside in the hot sun. We invited other non-caterers, such is our kindness, to hang out in our suite, drink some of our sodas, eat some leftovers. It turns out the guy in charge of the air-conditioning was a huge drag racing fan and told me much of what I'm telling you.

I can't for the life of me remember his name.

Anyway, after the first day I was going to write you a letter advising you to kill all the drag racing fans. It would've been really easy too because despite their $40 tickets everyone has to sit in these metal bleachers (except for the suiteholders of course). So I figured you could just wait for it to start raining. Hook up a few car batteries to the bleachers. 10,000 moustaches incinerated at once.

Now, after hearing the air-conditioning guy's story, I don't think that joke is funny anymore.

Earlier, he had told us that nobody is allowed to race when it's raining. That even the slightest water on the track can make a driver lose control of their car. What kind of guts does it take to be the first car to race after the rain delay? I showed up on the first day laughing at the stupid drag racers, and left after the third day with a grudging sense of respect.

They remind me of you, Al-Qaeda, in their commitment. Even if all they are is NASCAR drivers with ADD.

So during one of the rain delays, the air-conditioning guy in our suite told this story. He'd been telling us how he's seen every NHRA race here for the last eighteen years, whether he worked them or not. Then, I asked him if he'd ever seen one of these cars wreck.

Oh yeah . . . Yeah, I saw this one, but you probably don't want to hear about it. I mean some of y'all are still eating, and there's some ladies in the room.

We all insisted he tell the story.

Well, this one year, this was back in 1985 I think. I don't remember the guy's name, but he hits this spot of oil—and you gotta understand that it don't take no more but a spot— I mean just a drop of water, or a little pebble, and your car will go spinning off into next Tuesday. So something happened, I don't know if they ever found out for sure what, but anyway this guy loses control of his car. First it swerved to the left, and he kinda held it, but then it went back to the right and slammed into the wall and just . . . burst into flames. So he keeps going down the track, on fire, and the fire truck is already off after it before the guy's even done rolling to a stop. So now the car finally stops right about there—

He pointed to a spot by the chainlink fence at the end of the track.

—over by where the chainlink fence begins. And the guy jumps out, and he's just lit up like a fucking torch. And he's waving around and rolling on the ground, but there's just so much fuel in those things that once it blows it blows and there isn't nothing going to put it out except for some water. Now, the firetruck is parked next to him by this time, but in order to get their hoses hooked up they have to run them across the track, because back then they kept the water source over there on the right side of the track. So they run the hoses over and are rushing back, but by this point the ambulance is already hauling ass down there and on their way to the end of the track they end up running over the hose from the fire truck, so now the fire truck can't get no water.

Outside, the rain began to come down harder, forcing most of the bleachers to empty.

Well he just burned to death. Right there in front of us. There wasn't nothing anybody could do. It was . . . and I've seen a lot in this world–it was the most horrible thing I've ever seen. The agony that man was in, and all of us just sat there watching him. All these whole bleachers here was just people standing on their feet and watching. There was just this silence. It was the quietest thing. But–I shouldn't say this, but the one thing I will never forget is the smell. I hadn't never smelled burning flesh before. And the ambulance guys and the firemen were just standing there, not able to do anything, because if they grab him or anything they'll just end up burning right along with him. And it's just . . . y'know, I used to race all the time back then, but after that . . . I just couldn't do it. For a long time. And still, there's just something about that day. Every time I'm out here and it starts to rain.

Our suite remained silent, there was nothing to say. It's one thing to imagine how it might feel to be that ambulance driver, to inadvertently sever the hose that could have saved a man's life, to imagine what you would say to that man's family. It's another thing to talk about it.

Anyway, they moved the water source. They have about three or four of them out there now.

The rain began to let up. The fans returned to their seats– their wet, metal seats–the instant the storm lifted. What they were waiting to see, I hesitate to guess.

And on the last day as we were packing up, I made a joke to a redneck guy outside one of the suites. We had been loading the equipment out of the suite next door, and each time I went by. After my fourth or fifth trip he finally stopped me to ask, "Man, how much more shit you gotta carry out of here?"

I thought about the stories of fires and courage, the senseless deaths. Then I leaned my head into their suite and saw the stacked beercans on the tables and the cigarette butts smashed into the carpet. I looked him over slowly. After a few seconds, I grinned and said, "I don't know. How much do you weigh?"

His friends started laughing. I started laughing. And in the end he laughed, and added "fuck you."

You can say anything to anyone if you have a smile on your face.

Dear Al-Qaeda.

Everything is falling apart, yes I am.

The lampshade shivers in the air-conditioning and shakes its amber light. And I intend to figure this out if it takes the rest of the night.

I could pull her ribs out with a spoon and wag them beneath her open mouth, her eternally open & empty mouth.

For the sake of memory, which is faulty and prefers to remember feelings instead of details, the Christmas lights we purchased at Walgreen's had five different colors of bulb: pink, red, blue, green, orange. In that order, all the time.

I am resisting the urge to say what I am really thinking.

About love & hate, with their infinite slivers of difference.

I feel like throwing up.

Barf.

There is no 'I' in barf. I consider making a list of all the words that do not contain the letter 'I.'

you
me
us
here
now

fuck
you

This is easy.
I am, as the announcers say, beginning to heat up.

Soon I will be on fire.

Dear Al-Qaeda.

Nobody here will play chess with me so I play by myself.
I take turns, first white and then black. In the beginning, I
tried to play the same way for each player, not favoring
either one, but black just kept copying white's moves; so
white always won. Something had to be done, to relieve
the boredom, but I didn't know how to play any different
for black. Like any mediocre chess player, I have my
favorite moves–moves I prefer in certain situations–and I
didn't know how to choose a different strategy without
favoring either the white or black player.

For you see, fairness is important to me.

I decided to solve the problem by giving each player,
white and black, a distinct personality. To the white
player, I gave a spirit of generosity and benevolence. He
plays to win, but first and foremost he plays for the sheer
pleasure of playing. Sportsmanship and all that bullshit.
Even when he loses, he loses with a smile.

The black player is ruthless and seeks to destroy the white
player by any means necessary. When sitting in the black
player's chair, I often find myself cheating when the white
player is not in his seat.

And please don't read any kind of racial subtext into this
letter. White and black are merely colors meant to differ-
entiate, to keep the board from being all one color, and my
decision to personify black in such a manner can surely be
traced to a deep-seated anthropological fear of the night,
or black as the representation of death, and so what if the

black knight's horse has slightly larger lips? Jokes like that one are considered funny by bigots, as well as smart-asses. Which one do you think I am, Al-Qaeda?

Do you want to hear another racist joke?

Q: What do you call a black doctor?
A: A nigger.

Now these jokes might be going over your head, so allow me to explain them to you. Bridge the cultural gap as it were. The first joke, the one about the knight's horse, can be explained because generally speaking, black people have larger lips than white people. I'm not sure what's so funny about that, but then again I never liked Seinfeld either. As for the second joke, in the eyes of some people in this country, no matter how successful a black person becomes, they'll always be a nigger. Therefore a black doctor would still only be a nigger.

And this is a bad thing, in the eyes of bigots and black people, to get called a nigger.

Actually, in the eyes of some black people, it's even a bad thing to be called a black person. Some prefer to be called African-Americans. To complicate things further, I've met some blacks who think it's weird to be called African-American. So because we live in polite times, White America has decided to cover their multicultural asses and always refer to black people as African-Americans, presumably so they won't realize that White America still treats them like niggers.

I can think of two funny occurances as the result of White America's wholesale substitution of "A-A" for "Black." The first happened during the last Winter Olympics, when a black woman from the United States won a medal in bobsledding, leading to this priceless remark from one of the announcers. "We're certain she's the first African-American from the U.S. to medal in bobsledding, but we're still checking to see if any African-Americans from other countries have ever medaled in this event."

The second one happened when Pedro Martinez, of the 2004 world champion Boston Red Sox, was mentioned as one of the "few African-Americans to win a Cy Young Award." Pedro is from the Dominican Republic, neither African nor American, and Pedro hates being called either, for he is a Dominican.

Do you guys know any racial jokes about Kurds? Here, in the spirit of creating goodwill and further understanding between our two cultures, I'll write one for you.

Q: What shade of orange looks best on a Kurd?
A: Fire.

So when I play both sides of the chessboard, I actually feel different depending on which chair I'm sitting in. Like this whole other Scott appears, whether I'm in the white or the black chair. And you know what, Al-Qaeda, I've been playing like this every night for a month. The score is tied at fifteen and I still can't decide which side I like better. So I sit night after night, with Maya usually asleep in the other room of our two-room apartment, changing seats every few minutes and inflicting violence on the self who has just left his chair, which is me, which is myself. And tonight it occurs to me for the first time that maybe the only difference between victim and torturer is which chair you happen to be sitting in; that we all wear masks over our masks over ourselves until only the torture is real.

Or am I just stating the obvious.

Any insight you might have into this matter would be greatly appreciated.

Dear Al-Qaeda.

You may not see how this relates to you at first, but please hang in there. I promise the wait is worth it.

Last Sunday's *St. Petersburg Times* featured an article about a local entrepreneur named Ms. _____. She is the founder of a company called BumperNuts. If you're near the internet right now, you can go look up her website at www.bumpernuts.com. Why she didn't spell nuts with a 'z' is a mystery, for I truly think it would have put the final icing on the "what the fuck?" cake.

BumperNuts are made of foam rubber and fit securely on the trailer hitch on the back of one's pick-up truck. They are selling so fast that local stores can not keep these BumperNuts in stock. They are, as the saying goes, all the rage.

Oh yes, the foam rubber in BumperNuts has been molded to look like an oversized male ballsack.

Turns out we'd already seen a pair. Maya and I were driving on I-275. *Are those?* I asked. *Are they?* Maya wondered. It turns out they were.

The article was peppered with all the jokes one might expect. The guys who insist their real-life balls aren't nearly as big as the BumperNuts, the embarrassed wives and girlfriends who steal their man's BumperNuts and throw them in the garbage when he's not looking. Also, the BumperNuts come in different colors. According to the article, married men tend to prefer the blue ones. Get it, Al-Qaeda? Blue balls?

Another popular color is army camouflage, which is where you come in. One local Pinellas County resident shipped a pair to his son, who is currently fighting in Iraq. The son put them on the back of his tank, to let Iraqis know that Americans "have the balls to get the job done." The founder of BumperNuts, Ms. _____, swelled with pride while relating this story to the reporter.

I see on the news that some of you are in Iraq right now. Be careful, Al-Qaeda. I hear it's really dangerous there. Anyway, if you see a tank hurtling down the bombed-out streets of Baghdad with a large camouflaged set of testicles bouncing along on its back bumper, I thought you might like to know where they came from.

Though someday, thirty years from now, when we're looking back on all this war-on-terror shit as a distant memory, you may see a set of BumperNuts hanging in a shop window and freak the fuck out. Don't worry, Al-Qaeda. You're just experiencing a little psychological problem we in the west like to call Post-Traumatic Stress Disorder.

PTSD was in the news today because a lot of American soldiers are bringing it back with them when they come home from the war. That's how life is, I guess. Some soldiers' kids get t-shirts or postcards. Others get a father who dives for cover every time a car backfires. My dad brought PTSD back from Vietnam, along with exposure to something called Agent Orange. Twenty-five years after the fact, he still cowers under the bed whenever there is an earthquake.

To this day if someone is alone in a room, I clear my throat before I enter.

And oh yeah, he also has the diabetes and colon cancer

that come from exposure to Agent Orange. I assume these facts are left out of most military recruiting brochures.

I'm just wondering if twenty years down the road any of you might suffer from PTSD, Al-Qaeda. Or any Iraqis for that matter. Will you someday jump when your sons enter the room? To hear the doctors on the radio talk about it, this disease only seems to affect Americans. Because we're the more sensitive race, I assume.

Dear Al-Qaeda.

My use of the ampersand is always random & arbitrary. My index finger smells like a cross between earwax & tooth decay. I incessantly rub my fingers together until a waxy tartar ball begins to form. Sometimes I pull at my hair because I wish it was longer, and I dream of swallowing it all the way to the bottom.

Once upon a time in evolution–back when we still cared to evolve, when the future seemed worth showing up for, before classic rock & Nick at Nite & cotton candy became trinitized–we dreamed of losing our tails. And now that it's gone I want mine back. So I have something to chase instead of parked cars & pendulums, my pug nose crumpled & bleeding as I whimper on the sidewalk. I keep shitting on the grass in that space between the sidewalk and street, that foot-wide strip of lawn & landmines where we'd prefer not to step.

In the evening we throw our sweaters onto the floor. In the morning we throw our sweaters back onto the bed. I recognize the sunrise by the gradual lightening of sky, the rest is just a rumor, a faith I place in science.

Krispy Kreme donuts are the new communion. Burnt coffee tastes like the blood of our savior. After all, his Arab skin bled brown when pierced by the sword. Or so they taught me in Sunday school–that Arabs bleed different & blacks bleed better and white people bleed so we remember to cry.

I've found nothing worth crying for, Al-Qaeda. I laugh in the face of leprosy. Chuckle at the more cancerous forms of cancer. Schizophrenia is a joke found on bazooka gum wrappers. Castration is the funny papers. The expiration date is later than you think, and the riptide pulls tighter the harder you swim. Your arms become heavy; your head becomes lead.

We moved here five months ago & I'm still not sure why I'm here–is anyone ever sure about these things? I wanted to live here, but does anyone *really* live & why would they want to and if they did would I want to be their friend and do ideas like *want* even factor into the equation?

Weep like a pig, Al-Qaeda, for all the unread books and unanswered prayers. Someone dumped candy into the deep end of the pool and our children are collecting like stray pennies next to the drain. We've circled this beating bush long enough. I need your assistance, somebody please. I no longer like this learning to breathe through suffocation.

Dear Al-Qaeda.

In today's paper, the headline reads:

PRESIDENT TO RAISE
DECEASED BENEFIT TO $100,000

Which means that if you're an American soldier in Iraq and you die in combat, the government will now award your family a hundred grand. I read the headline in a newspaper box while walking back from dropping the rent check off at our landlord's. I didn't bring any change so I wasn't able to read the whole article, which means I can't tell you how much money our president might have paid the thousand or so families whose loved ones have already died.

A hundred grand isn't much, but if we compare it to your bereavement pay, Al-Qaeda, it flat out sucks. As I understand it, anyone who martyrs themselves for Al-Qaeda, aside from ascending immediately to heaven, will receive anywhere from fifty to five hundred virgins upon reaching the afterlife. This figure varies depending on who's telling the story.

Our soldiers are guaranteed nothing. Zip. Nada. Because once you're dead, what good is $100,000 going to do in the afterlife? As our grandparents used to say, you can't take it with you. No wonder our guys don't want to be over there. $100,000 won't support your family any longer than three or four years. Our soldiers can't go to heaven unless they've first accepted Jesus Christ as their personal savior. Atheist soldiers, Jewish soldiers, Mormons, etc. still receive eternal damnation, soldier or not.

And our lucky soldiers who make it into heaven won't even receive virgins, not a single one. Not that it would matter, because there is no sex in heaven and the only virgins died before they were twelve. Everyone just wears white togas and hangs out on clouds all day playing the harp. Which come to think of it sounds like most fraternities, except for the part about the harp.

Also, you get wings in heaven, but nobody seems to fly anywhere.

Dear Al-Qaeda.

I just want to do something for a job, something that I enjoy and I'm really good at. Just like our parents and teachers told us to do when we were kids.

I started writing fiction seriously, i.e. with the intent to publish for money, immediately after finishing school about two years ago. In that time, I completed a novel called *A Season in El Cajon*, a collection of stories set in the California hicktown where I grew up, as well as two novellas. *Scalpers: The Movie* is a book about a movie about ticket scalpers in Boston, and has just been made irrelevant by the recent Red Sox world series victory. The second novella is called *Just Call Me Snickers: by Sara "Snickers" Hannon*, a story about a girl who lives in a house with three roommates, and her too-strong identification with a cat that belongs to one of them. One day Snickers runs away from home, and in the process of searching for the cat, Sara inadvertently finds herself in the process.

I then wrote three-quarters of a novel, tentatively titled *Washing the Bones*, before junking it because I thought it sucked and didn't want to take the time to fix it.

I also have ideas for five additional novels, which I will share with you . . .

A Carolina Rebel in Larry Bird's Court
Our redneck protagonist has never been further north than downtown Asheville, won't even go to *north* Asheville such is his rebel pride. When his only brother dies suddenly–a brother who moved to Boston right out of high

school to get married–our redneck is forced to visit the cradle of Yankee culture. Hilarity ensues, with occasional pathos depending on my mood.

The Iraqnid

An epic poem concerning this country's fall from spiritual grace in the Persian Gulf, embodied by a Marine named Spider. His adventures far from home run parallel with his wife Caroline's domestic adventures. The mood of the country, spirals–the whole thing. Great American Novel, with a capital G A N.

Kick Me Out of the Ballgame

A collaboration between myself and my friend Alex in which we travel to every ballpark in the major leagues, then proceed to get kicked out in as undignified a manner as possible. Baseball, America, driving, and loss. Depending on our collective moods, could result in another Great American Novel, albeit this one's non-fiction.

Six Six Flags in Seven Days

A part-time waitress at Hooters and even parter-time student at UNC-Charlotte wins a radio contest. The prize: an all expense paid trip for two to a half-dozen Six Flags, to be completed in a week. Seeing she will travel to Dallas, she decides to track down a boy she fell in love with at cheerleading camp back in junior high school who used to live in Texas. Through the magic of the internet, they find one another and begin corresponding. Will they find true love? Will he look like a walrus?

The last book doesn't have a title yet, Al-Qaeda. It's a *DaVinci Code*-type thriller about an idealistic young woman who starts a new job at PETA (People for the Ethical Treatment of Animals). When she discovers some dark secrets lurking behind PETA's animal-friendly exterior she becomes outraged and decides to expose these secrets to the mass-media. When PETA gets wind of her plan, however, they decide to euthanize our heroine. Can she make it to the papers before the PETA zealots put her to sleep?

I haven't sent any of the completed books out, not because I'm modest or somehow afraid of failure, but because I'm broke. I've been broke for a long time. Not a pot to piss in, much less a window to throw it out of, as the saying goes. I'm hoping that we'll be able to save up enough money before we leave Florida that I can pay for photocopies and postage. It's been rough, Al-Qaeda.

Hey, aren't you guys supposed to be millionaires? Send me some cash. I could make you famous. Seriously.

Dear Al-Qaeda.

A tsunami struck parts of Southeast Asia a few days ago, killing 55,000 people in the process–or as I like to say, killing 18 times as many people who died on September 11th.

Now you might call this a tragedy. At the very least you'd probably call it sad. But then, you're not a Christian are you.

If you were a Christian, you might call the tsunami and its 55,000 deaths something else; you might call it justice.

This woman we work with, we'll call her "*Jesus*" in order to protect her identity, says the tsunami was just "God's way of killing the non-believers." Now I want you to understand, "*Jesus*" isn't some backwoods hick. "*Jesus*" is attending St. Petersburg College, a single mother, and in many ways is a better employee for Orange Blossom Catering than Maya or I will ever be. Even though all of us tried to reason with her, she continued to insist that those people died in the tsunami because they hadn't accepted Christ as their personal savior.

I mean who are the fanatics here, you or "*Jesus*?"

So I did a little research and discovered that only 33% of the world is Christian. And that number's on the decline. I want to make this clear: one of the tenets of Christian faith is that God is omnipotent. But if he's so fucking omnipotent, how can 2/3 of the world not believe in him? Either the Christian god isn't as all-powerful as we've been led to believe, or he's a slacker. And if you worked with "*Jesus*" like we do, you'd know she has no tolerance for slackers.

This number, this 33%, includes every denomination of Christianity. But once we start eliminating all the sects that "*Jesus*" doesn't agree with: the Mormons, the Catholics, Jehovah's Witnesses, Eastern Orthodox, Quakers, etc., we're left with a number around 4%. That's right. Not only does "*Jesus*" think that her God would murder 55,000 people who don't believe in Him, but that 96% of those still living will spend eternity in hell.

On a somewhat unrelated note, a third candidate ran for president during our last election. His name is Ralph Nader. When the other two presidential candidates debated, everyone agreed that Ralph shouldn't be allowed to participate because his share of the vote was too small to matter. Many people felt that Ralph shouldn't even be running for president, lest he take votes away from one of the two major candidates.

Ralph Nader ended up receiving about 4% of the vote in our election. If that number sounds familiar, it's the same percentage who believe in the same God that "*Jesus*" does–the one who kills people in Asia because they don't believe in him.

If she believes he is the most powerful god in the world, then she must also believe that Ralph Nader is the most powerful man in America.

And let the record show that, unlike the person who won the election, Ralph has yet to kill anyone.

Dear Al-Qaeda.

You may not be the right people to tell about this, but I'd be willing to bet that you can get my message to the right people. I need to talk about the price of gas here. This is ridiculous. We invade one of the most oil-rich countries on the planet, and the price of gas goes *up*. It nearly doubles. In some places, it nearly triples.

This is inconceivable to me. It's like invading Antarctica and having to pay more for ice cubes or penguin shit. And I'm as liberal as the next public radio listener, but I'd be a whole lot less against this war if the price of gas had gone down when we invaded Iraq.

Stability in the Middle East will aid U.S. interests. That's why we went to war in the first place. That's the reason we're stacking so many dead bodies that we need longer handles on our pitchforks in order to pluck them out of piles and throw them into their mass graves.

And the price of gas goes up.

I watch these cars and trucks on U.S. 19, the big purple vein that runs along the viagra-enhanced cock of Florida. It's six lanes of accidents waiting to happen and they usually do. Our cars get less miles per gallon now than they did before September 11th. Attack us again, Al-Qaeda, and we'll probably *all* start driving Hummers just to piss you off, Hummers with flag magnets and BumperNuts. We are a stubborn people, like mules, or jackasses if you prefer.

Oh hell, I can't think of any good words to describe us at the moment.

Freedom. We love freedom.

Dear Al-Qaeda.

There's an explanation for her mood swings.

The embryo was two months old. That is to say, the fetus was two months old.

Our baby was two months old.

It was floating yesterday afternoon; it is floating now even as I write this. It has moved with the current through the sewers, exchanging one saltwater home for another. Though it is only Spring, the Tampa Bay is already warm. She may even recognize its waters.

We did the right thing. To have this baby would mean staying in Florida, where Maya's parents are, indefinitely. We couldn't move to a new town, jobless, not knowing a single soul, and have a baby in six months, especially with no health care. I could apply for teaching jobs, but what if they said no? What if we were still catering? The fear, my god, the fear seems more real than the fetus did.

The baby.

And so she is gone. And we will never know what life she would have had. And we may never make another one again. And we can no longer look each other in the eye. And I do not know what to say.

I am sorry. To Maya, to our baby, and to myself. The truth is we are cowards.

They say you can't put a price on a child's life, but I beg

to differ. It costs exactly 385 dollars. I still have the receipt. I can show it to you.

Dear Al-Qaeda.

I went to Dunkin Donuts the other morning and got in line behind this old, sagging woman. She was ordering her donuts very seriously, like she was taking the SAT or buying a house, and not just a bunch of sugar and flour that will make her even fatter than she already is. Behind the counter stood a girl from a country not too far from yours. Obviously frustrated, she was strangling the life from her tongs and slumping her hips, the left hip nearly a foot higher than the right.

"You have seven donuts left," said the girl.
"Okay . . . let's see . . ."

In an effort to see the donut flavors, the woman strained her eyes as far as her skull would allow. I waited for an eyeball to pop out, bounce off her glasses, and roll around on the floor. Once it came to a stop, maybe some rat would scurry out, snatch it up in his jaws, and scamper back into his hole before the woman realized what had happened.

"Do you have any raspberry filled?" she asked.
"No. We are out."

"Are you sure? You don't have anymore in the back?"

"No, sorry, we had a very busy morning. No more raspberry filled."

"Not even in the back? Are you sure?"

"No more raspberry," the girl shook her head for emphasis.

The woman sighed. You could tell she didn't believe the girl and hoped that her sigh, her audible expression of want, would shame the girl into going into the back room and checking. She waited. I waited. The people gathering in line behind me waited. The cars at the stoplight behind us–where U.S. 19 intersects Gandy Blvd.–waited. Finally, the woman gave up.

"Well, in that case give me one of the crullers."
"Which cruller?"
"Which cruller?"
"Do you want the French or the blueberry?"
"Oh dear . . ." This set off more thoughts and considerations in the brain beneath her blue hair. "Let's see . . . I guess I'll take two of the French."

Somehow, at this point, for those of us in line, two donuts closer seemed like a miracle, a sprint towards the finish, a reason to be thankful.

The girl grabbed the donuts with her tongs and flung them into the box. The woman paused, then asked again,

"Are you sure you don't have any raspberry?"

The girl stared at her blankly, blinking occasionally, perhaps imagining a better world, or the satisfaction of thrusting her thumbs into the woman's eye sockets.

"No, I guess not. Well, just give me . . . two old-fashioned . . ."
"Three more," snapped the girl.
"One blueberry–can I get a blueberry muffin? Does that count?"
"No. Only donuts."
"No?"
It was the girl's turn to sigh. "You can, but you must pay separate. Not part of the dozen."
"Oh dear . . . well, I guess a blueberry donut then–"
"Two more."

The woman rubbed her fingers over her chin, where I could see a thin, black hair beginning to sprout. It made me think of the three little pigs. She appeared to be fondling–or milking–it.

"Give me another cimmanon."

"*Cinnamon.*"

"That's what I said," snapped the woman.

The girl rolled her eyes. "You have one more donut, ma'am."

"Hm . . . what to do . . . I just don't . . . hm . . ."

I looked over my shoulder, past the sunburnt construction worker behind me, shifting his weight from side to side, past the girl in sweatpants and the toddler that was either her daughter or her little sister–it was just too close to call–past the rest of the faceless Floridians, and out to U.S. 19, where the traffic was now on its seventh stoplight since I'd gotten in line.

I suddenly realized that this is the fourth time I have lived on or near this state route.

The first time occurred when I was 8. Shortly after the divorce, my mom decided it would be good to live closer to her family so we moved to Plains, Georgia, birthplace of the 39th President of the United States, Jimmy Carter. Plains had a population of 600, and the school system left a lot to be desired. For what it's worth, I was one of five white kids in the entire school. And due to my grand-mother's *traditions*, none of my black friends were allowed in our house. Technically, I wasn't supposed to be friends with them in the first place.

We left Georgia when I was 10, but I moved back after I dropped out of college for the second time, when I was 19. I lived in my grandmother's house again while I worked for Cooper Lighting in a factory as a machine press operator. I made fluorescent light fixtures. I liked it.

During my time in Georgia, U.S. 19 was the route you took to go to Albany, where the nearest bookstore was located. Albany is 40 miles south of Plains.

My last encounter with U.S. 19, before I came here to Florida, was in Asheville, North Carolina, where I was living when Maya came to visit me, to see if we were finally going to jump off that bridge we'd been circling for the last couple of years. During her week in Asheville, we fell in love with each other. I was already out of love with Asheville, so I had no problem following her wherever our love might take us.

It has brought us to Florida, where U.S. 19 is the most dangerous stretch of road in the area. People die on it every day. Old people who are on so much prescription medicine they can hardly see straight.

Our love brought us to Florida, and the hunger created by that love had brought me to Dunkin Donuts, though I doubt donuts will satisfy my hunger any more than Maya has been able to lately.

"For my last donut . . ." She snaps me out of my day-dream. We are no closer to the end. "How about . . . if I have . . . for my last donut, oh just give me another old-fashioned."

The girl shoves the donut into the box and folds it shut in one motion. "That will be six dollars and twenty-three cents."

The woman pulls a pink wallet from a large straw bag that could be used as a suitcase.

Dollar bill.
Five dollar bill.
Dime.
Nickel.
Penny.
Penny.
Nickel.
Penny.

As the girl collects the money, the woman tilts her head back and narrows her gray eyes.

"What are those over there on that tray?" She gestures towards several racks of donuts lurking back in the kitchen.

"Those are . . . donuts," answers the girl.

"Well do you have any raspberry filled back *there*?" She speaks slowly, like someone addressing a child, a child they think is retarded.

"No. I told you we have no raspberry."

"Hm. Well, I guess if you say so."

Are you following all of this, Al-Qaeda? This woman, this fucking liver-spotted beast of a human being, thought the Dunkin Donuts person was actually *lying* to her. I guess because donut people try really hard *to purposely not sell their donuts*, like out of spite or something. There's nothing sacred about these raspberry donuts; they're not filled with the blood of this girl's son. They were donuts.

A sharp rain began to fall as the woman shuffled out to her car. I rooted for her to slip in a puddle and fracture her chalk-like skull, but she just opened the door and got into an Oldsmobile Cutlass. Pulling into traffic, a truck had to slam on its brakes to avoid hitting her, and in this process her life was spared.

Justice was not done, Al-Qaeda. I am asking you to set things right.

I don't know this woman's name. She had a bumper sticker on her car. *God Bless America* was written on a ribbon colored like the American flag. I understand this doesn't narrow it down a whole lot. Please pray to Allah. Find out who this woman is. She needs to be stopped. She has nothing to live for. Some people might argue she's someone's grandmother, but I promise you she is mean and her grandchildren probably view a visit to this woman's house the way most of us look forward to driving through Texas.

She is old; she is withered like a bird. She deserves not to die from natural causes.

Dear Al-Qaeda.

Here's an ad from this week's edition of the *Weekly Planet*, Tampa Bay's free alternative newspaper:

> *WHITE COUPLE 50+ she, 5", 105lbs, sexy, blonde. Seeking 1 clean, slim, circumcised, educated, preferably Jewish, under 35 male for occasional satisfaction of wife. Must love giving her oral sex. Into spanking and role play.*

What the fuck is this all about? I want you to eat out my wife, but I'd prefer you to be Jewish? Isn't there a war going on with soldiers coming home in body bags, Arabs up to their necks in blood, and you're telling me this guy's main concern is foreskin? And he can't even tell the difference between feet and inches.

We are a dying decadent piece of shit society.

He has a box number if you wish to contact him. Or you can wait until next month, after Maya and I have already left, and then waste the whole fucking state. Spank him good, Al-Qaeda. Hijack another plane and spank the fuck out of him. Spank him until he's dead.

Dear Al-Qaeda.

We will be leaving Florida on schedule, in about a month, but we will not be leaving for the same place. We no longer belong together, Maya and I. This not fun anymore. I am beginning to question if it ever was.

I was the one to say it. *I think we should break up.* Do I earn extra points for this? Maybe. I told some people at work. The guys couldn't understand. *But dude, she's so hot.* The girls, without exception, assume that I am cruel.

Somebody broke up with them once, that is all they need to know.

Will I miss her? I've been missing her for some time now. It's tempting to list all her faults in one neat little list, like I once listed the seven deadly sins to you, or Tampa's favorite death metal bands, but she deserves better than that. Maya was never the enemy, and if she offends me now it's only because there's no other way forward. We have to go forward. Our love has not grown cold, only taciturn.

It's easy, when someone looks deeply into your eyes and tells you that they love you–that you are absolutely perfect for them and they want to have your children. It's easy to not see the landmines all around you. To see them as speedbumps, or even worse, as cute and charming.

If not happy, I was at least content.

I will love her again eventually. Differently, in a manner more deep and infinitely more shallow.

But for now I don't wish to see her. Or you, or anyone.

Dear Al-Qaeda.

I hear she has found someone else now, someone more bright & sparkly, and altogether sunnier than I am. Sunnier, it seems, than I will ever be.

She can say it's not serious; it certainly feels serious enough to me.

Dear Al-Qaeda.

I'm tired of this. I look everywhere, and all I find is con-
fusion.

Let's approach this from another direction. I'll bet you've
never heard of Clara Bow. She was a famous actress in the
1920's. If I wanted to insult Clara's talent, I might call her
the Courtney Love of her day. Her biography is my mouse
pad. It sits on top of a book about a seminal music group
called Pavement. They don't exist anymore, and you've
never heard of them either.

Which is to say that all of this is just anonymous and bullshit and pointless.

I don't understand why you even try, Al-Qaeda. Crusading
for what? Religion? God? Because the United States
threw the first punch? Your answer to everything is death.

Yet death is inevitable. Kill someone, and all you've done
is shorten their lifespan, a lifespan that only would have
been spent turning oxygen into carbon dioxide, eating
three meals a day, praying on the sabbath, and maybe
producing a few more human beings to engage in the same
pointless cycle.

I don't know what's more pointless, to mourn those whose
lives were cut short, or to cut your own life short in order
to avenge their deaths. Dust, it is all fucking dust, Al-
Qaeda. There is no cause worth dying for. The only point
of life is to live.

I used to believe that if someone attacked the United

States, I would risk my life in order to defend it; I no longer believe this.

The point of life is to live.

Death is the only thing that can keep me from living. For all our talk of Freedom, life everywhere is pretty much the same. Wake up, go to some shitty job, come home, repeat. That won't change no matter who runs the world, no matter which flag we salute. Most of us just want to be left alone so we can savor the few fleeting moments of freedom and pleasure that come between all that waking and working.

As for that cherished American Freedom, I am here to say that it is nothing more than the freedom to agree with one's neighbors.

And as far as the whole 'likely to get me killed' thing goes, you're probably tied with my own government at this point. With the war on terror seeming to actually increase the number of dead Americans, I'm not sure what to think anymore.

Let's drop the act, Al-Qaeda. Mankind is a virus. We are no better than a flock of pigeons. Nothing more than an anthill, an anthill that likes to wear baseball caps.

What is there to give our lives meaning?

Live for love?
> Love is a death camp at the center of a lollipop.

Live for art?
> All art is either misunderstood or forgotten.

Live for god?

> He won't love you until you cease to live.

Live for your country?

> It will repay that love by sending you off to die for no good reason.

Live for your job?

> You'll get a watch at 65 and a retirement party at Outback Steakhouse.

Live for the weekend?

> In order to enjoy it, you'll have to work five days a week at some job you hate, a job that will leave you so tired that you spend the weekend–the one you worked for–drinking beer on the sofa.

So what is left?

> Nothing.

Nothing. One big nothing upon nothing. Your Allah is nothing, Al-Qaeda. Your turbans are nothing. Your silly little beards are nothing. And you would die, happily, for all of it. For nothing. You shouldn't read these letters. Nobody should. These letters are nothing. This country is nothing. I am nothing. And once you start down this rabbit hole all you find is mad hatters and playing cards who shout *Off with his head!* and can't somebody please find me a sweeter cup of tea.

Enemies are imaginary and all of our friends will eventually say goodbye.

We get lost in our fright, and when we do just remember to sing sha-la-la-la-la.

Remember that even in winter, the heart still longs to atone.

We are surrounded by lives and possibilities that we will never even imagine, but we spend our days like pigeons and kittens, chasing stray peanuts or sleeping away the afternoon on down comforters.

We could stop killing each other though, I'm certain of that.

But I am finished caring. All my caring has gotten me is tired; I want to sleep.

Please don't write back.

Your friend,
Scott

Scott Creney no longer lives in Florida.